"An accessible and efficient introduction to the strategy for university students of all levels of study.

—Dr. Joel Deichmann, Professor of Global Studies, Bentley University, Massachusetts, United States.

"Johnson's text provides a solid basis to understand and develop a global strategy…. He walks the reader through emergent and deliberate strategies in an array of cultural settings. On the build, borrow, or buy question, Johnson's treatment is as thoughtful as any I have seen. Examples elucidate concepts and will surely stick in the minds of students. In addition to laying out a solid foundation, Johnson does not shy away from bringing in nuances and layering on necessary complexity."

— Dr. Scott C. Ensign, Associate Professor of Policy, Dobson Professor of Innovation and Entrepreneurship, Lazaridis School of Business & Economics, Canada.

"In today's interconnected world, even the smallest businesses have easy access to tools that allow them to operate globally, from online communication and data-sharing tools to international financial instruments to crowdsourcing and marketplace platforms. What they often lack is a global strategy. Professor Johnson's textbook provides an in-depth, yet easy-to-follow guide for the new generation of entrepreneurs and managers seeking to develop a strategy for global expansion, from market analysis to management of human resources."

—Dr. Vasyl Taras, X-Culture Founder and Project Director, Associate Professor of Management, Bryan School of Business and Economics, University of North Carolina at Greensboro, United States.

"When I teach business strategy, I do it to develop in my students an international vision of possibilities and threats. This book explains what it means to strategize in the global context that they will be in. I value the approach of developing strategy, with its unplanned emergent aspects, rather than imagining it as something to be selected from several items on a shelf. The book pushes students to be practical and realistic. Examples from all types of firms—software, big box, not-for-profit etc.—is enriching…. The book is rich in tools for analysis of both internal and external factors. These are accompanied by suggestions in how to best employ them at all organization levels and contexts in a most compelling way. As someone who values top student evaluations, I see adopting this book as integral to my teaching strategy."

— Dr. Charles Wankel, Professor of Management, Peter J. Tobin College of Business, St. John's University, USA.

Managing Global Strategy

This concise, practical textbook clearly explains how to go about developing and implementing a global strategy for any organization, from Born Global start-ups, to more established large companies struggling to manage their global extensions, to nonprofits including non-governmental organizations (NGOs) and charities.

Written clearly and concisely, this volume brings together multiple tools, models and frameworks into one resource to guide a successful global strategy development and implementation process. Issues covered include:

- Internal and external environmental analyses;
- Cross-cultural communication;
- Structural considerations;
- Leadership and motivation;
- Foreign market entry, mergers, alliances and acquisitions.

Upper-level undergraduate and postgraduate students of global business will appreciate this accessible guide to a highly complex endeavor, as will practicing managers in global organizations seeking a ready reference. Instructors will also value the outline of a semester-long project keyed to the book, developed and tested by the author.

William H. A. Johnson is Associate Professor of Management at Pennsylvania State University Behrend, Erie, United States. His research and teaching are at the nexus of innovation, strategy and international management.

Managing Global Strategy

Developing an Effective Strategy in International Business

WILLIAM H. A. JOHNSON

Routledge
Taylor & Francis Group

NEW YORK AND LONDON

First published 2021
by Routledge
52 Vanderbilt Avenue, New York, NY 10017

and by Routledge
2 Park Square, Milton Park, Abingdon, Oxon OX14 4RN

Routledge is an imprint of the Taylor & Francis Group, an informa business

Library of Congress Cataloging-in-Publication Data
Names: Johnson, William H. A., author.
Title: Managing global strategy : developing an effective
strategy in international business / William H. A. Johnson.
Description: New York : Routledge, 2020. |
Includes bibliographical references and index.
Identifiers: LCCN 2020019801 (print) | LCCN 2020019802 (ebook) |
ISBN 9780367468552 (hardback) | ISBN 9780367462857 (paperback) |
ISBN 9781003031529 (ebook)
Subjects: LCSH: International business enterprises–Management. |
Strategic planning. | Intercultural communication. |
Diversity in the workplace–Management.
Classification: LCC HD62.4 .J454 2020 (print) | LCC HD62.4 (ebook) |
DDC 658.4/012–dc23
LC record available at https://lccn.loc.gov/2020019801
LC ebook record available at https://lccn.loc.gov/2020019802

ISBN: 978-0-367-46855-2 (hbk)
ISBN: 978-0-367-46285-7 (pbk)
ISBN: 978-1-003-03152-9 (ebk)

Typeset in Dante MT Std
by Newgen Publishing UK

Contents

Figures

Tables

Preface

I wrote *Managing Global Strategy* to provide my students at the Black School of Business, Penn State University, Erie—the Behrend College with a concise book that demonstrates the basic models and frameworks developed by business strategists and applies them to foreign investments at the organizational level. Although there are some excellent textbooks that discuss strategy and international management, separately and sometimes together, most are either too comprehensive or missing small but important topics to be useful for my teaching objectives. Consequently, the book stems from my desire to have a text that helped my university-level international business (IB) students map out an approach to developing an organization's strategy for going abroad. I focused on the essential material used to guide the exploration of pertinent issues for developing the global strategic plan for any organization. As such, I do not include all fundamental and basic aspects of either disciple (i.e., strategy or IB). For example, I assume that my IB students already know something about exchange rate risk, global supply chains, international logistics and other general aspects of strategy and all the business functions, etc. To some extent, I assume that too of the casual reader, and emphasize the necessary structural elements of strategy at the global level to create a unique plan of his or her own based on further research by the reader.

My school also emphasizes practice over theory, so, while I use conceptual generalizations in the models and frameworks presented (which, as an academic, I find very useful for universal application), I also try to communicate it all in an experiential way to business students, who tend to think pragmatically. Thus, the book uses an experiential approach. Via the research that they do individually and in teams (using the book as their guide), my students learn much more than I could fit into such a small book. Instead they develop a better understanding of strategic planning at the global level by means of the specific information they discover in their chosen context (i.e., company, country, etc.). Essentially, the book is meant as a guide to help the reader create more knowledge via their own research and not as a static depository of knowledge in which a passive reader need only engage in its pages. The learning only just begins after reading the book and when the reader explores more on their own.

I intentionally kept discussion / analysis in the book to be simple rather than complex and focus mostly on the general development and implementation issues of strategy. Specific trade and business policies as well as legal and cultural aspects will differ across any of the 193 or so countries of the world, so this is primarily left to the student and reader to "research" on their own (or in a class as a team and "report" back to the teacher about their findings). In my case, I have domestic US students as well as international students in my classes but, being at an American university, most of my student teams take on an American perspective / company and discuss entry into another foreign country (though not always; for example, I've had a group use Toyota as their "company" and take the perspective of Japan as the "home" country). My point here is that the book is written to be universal in scope (albeit most management theories used are Western-biased), whereby generic strategic management concepts can be used in any context to help analyze the business environment and begin to create a strategy for implementation by applying the specific contextual elements of that business environment. The context will dictate which are more important than others.

Students today tend to read less, but they still need to know the fundamentals in such a way that they can do something with the frameworks at hand. This is the experiential aspect to the book, and it is with that philosophy that I approached writing it. I wanted to dwindle down the information to the essence of what one needs to know in order to develop an effective strategy. I believe that the result is a concise primer that anyone can use to structure their thinking about the issues of developing an organization's global strategy—particularly using a meticulous process that requires the analyst to be precise about each element of the models used. It is not meant to be a comprehensive textbook on IB or strategy but, rather, a succinct melding of both topics needed to effectively create a foreign business strategic plan.

As a result, the book makes an excellent required textbook for modules or courses that focus specifically on global strategy, such as my own at Penn State University—backed up perhaps with supplemental readings that may be pertinent to the specific contexts of the course.

At the same time, any interested reader or practitioner can use the book as a guide when thinking about the process of researching, developing and implementing such a plan. Careful thinking is necessary here. As I argue in the strategy sections of the book, many practitioners' strategies have failed due to lack of precise definitions and logic—essentially, analysis that suffers from the garbage in, garbage out (GIGO) phenomenon. As a result, practitioners would be wise to follow the structured approach I offer here.

Finally, the book might also be used as a supplemental text for either a general strategy or an IB course with a multi-component project that combines strategy and IB issues and is best completed over the entire semester (as described in the book's Appendix, and for which supplemental material may be provided by Routledge eResources to help instructors needing a little more material to bring into the classroom).

Note on Covid-19

As I was in the pre-production stage of completing the book, the Covid-19 pandemic struck. Unfortunately, the Covid-19 tragedy will likely result in slow to stagnant economic growth, particularly across international borders. Global trade is already negatively affected. This may lead people to ask the questions whether global business is doomed and whether developing a global strategy is still needed. Fortunately, the answer is still "Yes". In fact, this may be the best time to learn how to do it right, so that one is ready for when growth happens. The increase in global trade and investments since the Second World War has resulted in the largest growth in wealth and security in the history of the world. Granted, there are winners and losers, and not everything about globalization has been positive, but the history of mankind has shown that we are better off as a species when we are interacting fairly and actively with each other. In fact, man is not the strongest animal or the largest or most hardy, but a distinguishing feature of humanity has been its ability to adapt, communicate and cooperate among individual actors, which leads to innovation and adaptation. Global trade is not new and will not end with the pandemic (though some processes and attitudes will change). Precursors of the multinational organization, such as the British East India company, also experienced wars, famine and disease and still survived through them—and so will modern global business. From the ashes of the viral disease will come opportunities and threats that need to be analyzed from an organizational perspective.

In fact, it occurs to me that, although this book is written for the business student and from the perspective of free enterprise, most of the ideas contained herein, with regard to strategy development and enactment, can be applied to any situation needing strategic analysis. That is, the concepts of strategy in terms of "the logic that ties all decisions and actions together" can be used in disaster response initiatives, development of appropriate responses to viral outbreaks and any other such endeavor that involves managing a response through coordinated actions. But, of course, this is beyond the scope of this book.

Covid-19 will change the world, but we will survive as a species through this trial. With hope, we will come out stronger and see that the coming together of global actors for the good of the world through shared benefits and growth is a necessary part of our mutual survival. A combination of cooperation and competition is needed; too much of the latter is counter-effective. Closing borders does not make us safe; opening minds, to better understand each other, does (at least as a start).

Acknowledgements

As with all endeavors in life, this book would not be possible without the help and encouragement of others. In particular, I express my greatest gratitude to Ruth Benner, for being there to bounce ideas off and for helping me design some of the graphics used in the book. Those who know her know that she is an amazing person. I am forever grateful to have her in my life.

I would like to thank the editors and others at Routledge who have helped me along the publication path for this book—notably Meredith Norwich, Sophia Levine and, especially, Emmie Shand, who helped with the nitty-gritty parts that get the job done in the end. In addition, my gratitude goes to three anonymous reviewers of the first draft of the book, who provided valuable feedback and helped me make the focus of the book clearer. As a practicing academic, I know the importance and also frustration of reviewer feedback (e.g., when different reviewer comments sometimes seem to contradict each other, etc.), but I have always found the process of peer review leads to a superior outcome whenever such feedback results in rethinking a project. I am glad that Routledge utilizes such peer review in its publication process.

Finally, I would like to thank my students in the international business program at the Black School of Business, Penn State University, Erie—the Behrend College. Many of them provided feedback on initial drafts of the book. All of them helped in the learning experience of understanding how to approach the analysis and implementation of global business strategies from the learners' perspective.

Part 1

Setting the Context

Introduction to Strategy in a Global Context **1**

Learning Objectives

By the end of this chapter, you will:

- Understand what is meant by strategy and, in particular, strategy in a global context;
- Appreciate what the external aspects of strategy are and how they are useful in developing strategy;
- Appreciate what the internal aspects of strategy are and how they are useful in developing strategy;
- Comprehend how strategy can be used to manage the process of globalization for an organization.

Practice Objectives

By the end of this chapter, you will be able to:

- Define the basic aspects of strategy for an organization that is either for-profit or not-for-profit;
- Define the hierarchy of strategies within a complex organization;
- Identify an existing public company and describe its strategy and global perspective.

Imagine that you are an entrepreneur who has successfully developed a new product that you believe can be sold worldwide. For expository purposes, let's assume that it's a new software app that with the power of the internet and social media can be marketed and sold anywhere in the world. As such, you want to make sure that you can benefit from as much exposure as possible, and you decide to take your newly formed company global. That is, you are the proud owner / manager of a Born Global company—one that is simultaneously domestic and foreign right from the time of its inception. So, what are the management issues that you need to understand to be successful?

This primer is about answering that question and explaining how to go about preparing your company for success. Notably, it's also about preparing you and your company team for the issues that you will encounter along your journey towards implementing a successful global strategy. It is important to point out that, before we get to the specific global / international issues we will confront, we must first understand a little about the basic elements and concepts of strategy. (We'll get to defining strategy a little later.)

Many of these issues will be appropriate for larger, more established companies as well—such as Fortune 500 giants Walmart and Amazon. The same goes for not-for-profit organizations. As we will see throughout the book, context is important for understanding what things need to be focused on and what things are less important. However, in the end, the basic frameworks that have been useful for strategy and management in organizations can be applied in almost all of the situations you encounter. It is just the specific details that may be different. For example, a not-for-profit organization will still need to define its "reason for existing" and develop a strategy for sustaining itself, just as a for-profit firm must do. The major difference is the lack of a profit motive being paramount to the success of the not-for-profit firm.

Here are three different examples of organizations that are of interest to us. We can apply each of the tools, models and frameworks discussed in this book for each organizational situation. The first example is a situation similar to the company mentioned in the first paragraph above—the small entrepreneurial Born Global company. The second example is of larger, more established companies such as the Walmarts and Amazons of the world, which may already have extensive global reach but are still struggling with managing those extensions properly. Finally, because not all organizations that exist and perform important duties are for-profit, the last example are situations involving not-for-profit organizations, like non-governmental organizations such as Doctors Without Borders and the Red Cross, or charitable organizations like the United Way.

Note that, throughout the book, the terms "company", "firm", "enterprise" and "organization" are meant to be similar in nature but with subtle differences. The first three terms are consistent with for-profits and are specific in nature. The latter term is more general and is useful for also including not-for-profits and governmental entities. As such, I use "organization" when referring to the general concept of an entity managed by managers (whether not-for-profit or for-profit) and the other terms when being more specific.

The Normative Imperative

Many of the frameworks, models, ideas, etc. that are useful in managing organizations are based on various perspectives of "viewing" the way things *should be done*. This is a normative approach: It's about how things "should be" done based on logic and experience (i.e., of situations that appear to lead to a higher probability of success). The important thing to note is that this is not necessarily how things are actually done in practice. That is, based on careful analysis, we can determine what should be done for an organization and offer a strategy as the basis for action. This does not mean that the organization will enact that strategy nor does it mean that things will not change to create a need for a different strategy. This explains how some successful companies of the past can often become examples of what not to do when the (environmental) context of their success changes.

Strategy is complex and enacted over time (usually a long time)—so it is difficult to see how everything fits together and creates success at any single point in time. As shown in the matrix of Table 1.1, while strategy can lead to successful outcomes for an organization through the logical implementation of its premises, luck can also play a role in some successful outcomes. However, normatively (that is, a logical approach based on experience and practice), long-term success is possible only with an appropriate strategy that links external aspects of the (competitive) environment with the organization's internal resources and capabilities to create and manage a efficient and determined effort. So, let's look at these concepts in more detail …

Levels of Management

There are two basic levels of management issues for any organization, and we will follow this logic throughout this book. The first is the macro level. As the name implies, it deals with issues that are large in nature and general to

Table 1.1 Contingencies towards success

		/----------------Strategy----------------\			
		Well done	Well done	Poorly done	Poorly done
Implementation	Well done	*Ultimate success*	*Temporary setback*	*Temporary success*	*Turnaround candidate*
	Poorly done	*Temporary success*	*Difficult to succeed*	*House of cards*	*Total failure*
		Good	Bad	Good	Bad
		\----------------Luck----------------/			

the organization. As such, dealing with macro issues is also sometimes called general management (hence the term "general manager" as the CEO, usually used for smaller firms). Macro issues are at the strategic level and may include such questions as these: In what businesses/practices is the organization going to be involved; how will it manage external factors towards success in those businesses/practices? Thus, the macro level is about managing the main goals of the organization and the "general" methods of obtaining them.

The second basic level of management for any organization is the micro level. This tends to be at the operational perspective and tends to follow from the macro issues of strategy in terms of implementation. Micro-level issues involve the management of people and the structural framework of an organization—generally, human resources (HR) and organizational structure issues. Thus, the micro level is about implementing the macro strategy, and therefore (while ideally based on that strategy) is *operational* in nature.

These two levels are conceptual frameworks for studying the complex relationships within the globalized organization. (That is, they help us "slice and dice", or compartmentalize, the organization into parts so that we can study it and more easily understand what's going on.) In general, the macro issues logically come first in the creation and communication of effective strategy, which we will, naturally, study first in this book. The micro issues normatively follow from the chosen strategy of the organization—that is, how to manage the people and partners of the organization, where to place various operations in the world, etc. What makes it even more interesting in the global context is that culture and foreign institutions, such as the courts of law and governments of other countries, bring their own unique challenges to the "macro-level" strategy of an organization. The global context provides context-dependent management principles and actions, and it is the handling of these issues that constitutes the backbone of this book. The book itself is your guide to continue researching and studying these context-specific issues via internet and library research for whatever specific strategic path you choose (i.e., country and company / organization of interest).

What Is Strategy?

Now let's get to what strategy is … There are a multitude of definitions for strategy. (See Table 1.2 for a sample of some of the great thinkers on strategy). In general, all the mainstream definitions include elements of goals, methods and, ultimately, success. That is, strategy is the long-term overarching process towards successfully achieving the major goals of the organization. Going back to the notion of normative reasoning mentioned earlier, my general definition of strategy is "the logic inherent in every major decision made within the organization". This is because, ideally, every decision made *should* (again, here's the normative imperative!) relate to the ultimate goal(s) of the organization (though they often do not, and that constitutes bad strategy!).

Think of it as if everyone and everything in the organization should be going in the same direction. For example, which relay bike team in Figure 1.1 do you think will win the race? The one with a straight path or the one that rides all over the place and in different directions? When everyone is aligned towards the overall goals of the organization, they are likely to be more successful (again, luck and execution will also play a part: recall Table 1.1).

The actual actions taken towards achieving success are best thought of as tactics (or mini-strategies) that lead towards the ultimate goals of the organization. Strategies tend to be "big picture"-type perspectives. Another way to look at strategy is that it encompasses the *raison d'être*, or "reason for being",

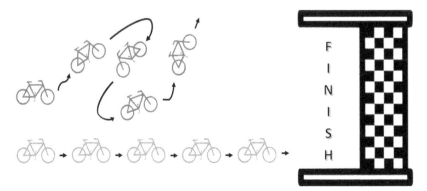

Figure 1.1 Strategy: like a bike race

Table 1.2 Select definitions of strategy from well-known strategic management experts over time

Definition of strategy	Source
Strategy is the great work of the organization. In situations of life and death, it is the Tao of survival or extinction. Its study cannot be neglected.	Sun Tzu. *The Art of War* (5th century BC)
Strategy is what matters for the effectiveness of the organization, the external point of view, which stresses the relevance of the objectives against the environment, in terms of internal stresses, the balanced communication between members of the organization and a willingness to contribute towards actions and the achievement of common objectives.	Barnard (1938)
Strategy is a series of actions undertaken by a company according to a particular situation.	Von Neumann & Morgenstern (1947)
Strategy is analyzing the present situation and changing it whenever necessary. Incorporated within this is finding out what one's resources are or what they should be.	Drucker (1954)
Strategy is the determinant of the basic long-term goals of a firm, and the adoption of courses of action and the allocation of resources necessary for carrying out these goals.	Chandler (1962)
Strategy is a set of rules for decision making under conditions of partial ignorance. Strategic decisions concern the firm's relationship with its ecosystem.	Ansoff (1979)
Strategy is a mediating force between the organization and its environment: consistent patterns in streams of organizational decisions to deal with the environment.	Mintzberg (1979)
Strategy is the pattern of decisions that guide the organization in its relationship with the environment, affect the processes and internal structures, as well as influencing the performance of organizations.	Hambrick (1980)
Strategy is the company choice as to key decision variables such as price, promotion, quantity and quality. The company, to have good performance, must be correctly positioned in its industry.	Porter (1980)
Strategy is to define the direction of organizations. This includes issues of primary concern to the manager, or any person who seeks the reasons for success and failure between organizations.	Rumelt, Schendel & Teece (1994)
Strategy is a set of plans or decisions made in an effort to help organizations achieve their objectives.	Miller & Dess (1996)

(*continued*)

Table 1.2 (Cont.)

Definition of strategy	Source
Strategy means performing different activities to those performed by rivals or performing the same activities differently.	Porter (1996)
Strategy is the theory of the firm on how to compete successfully. It also considers performance as a factor influenced by strategy, as it can be considered that to compete successfully means having a satisfactory performance.	Barney (2001)

of an organization. As such, I also like using the concept of strategy as "the philosophy of an organization". Just as a personal philosophy can be seen as an all-encompassing way of living, so too can a business strategy be seen as an all-encompassing way of doing business. Your personal philosophy helps determine your actions, and this is also the case for organizations in business strategy. Of course, you don't have to be totally philosophical to be a great strategist, but it may help. Many of the great strategists were philosophers like the *Art of War* philosopher Sun Tzu, and, like him, their philosophical treatises often involved the concept of war and peace.

Types/Levels of Strategy

There is a hierarchy of strategy in most large organizations that have multiple organizational units, and this will be even more pronounced in globalized organizations. For businesses, this results in the first layer of corporate strategy, which is about answering the question "What types of businesses will we invest in as a corporation?". Usually here the logic behind investing in various businesses is based on underlying corporate core competences that can be utilized across the various units. Again, the notion of a normative perspective is important here. As we'll see in later chapters, not all investments make sense, and they can often lead to underperformance. However, this is merely bad strategic formulation, akin to what was shown as a potential option in Figure 1.1. When the logic linking decisions is bad this means by definition that the strategy itself is bad. For example, we might have chosen the wrong business to buy on a false premise of some underlying competence or skill set that we really don't have.

The second layer of the strategy hierarchy is business strategy, which answers the question "As an individual business, how will we compete to achieve our strategic goal(s)?". In other words, what will be the underlying logic for the decisions we make at the business unit level?

As you can see, the difference between these levels of strategy really has to do with organizational level. Corporate involves multiple units; business involves one sole unit. We often refer to such a unit as the strategic business unit (SBU). We can translate a similar type of hierarchy to the not-for-profit scenario, where an organization may consist of multiple units. An example would be the large charity organization the United Way, which is a conglomerate of various smaller charities like the Salvation Army and Big Brothers Big Sisters of America that could be viewed just like business units or SBUs—just not with a major objective of creating profit! So why does this corporate structure exist for the United Way? Namely, the core competence of the larger entity of the United Way is its ability to raise funds for charity while each individual charity has its own unique goal(s) to achieve.

Within an SBU we can also break down units into various functional levels. This is often done to create individual functional-level strategies. While this may work and be okay, I urge caution when referring to functional actions as strategies, because they should not be enacted in isolation of the main SBU's business strategy. The strategies of two SBUs within a single corporation might be quite different. That is, the logic of decision-making and the success defined for any two SBUs can be quite different and therefore may be managed differently. However, functions within a single SBU, like marketing or production, must be aligned for optimal success. Think of the functions as the individual members of a team and the SBUs as actually different teams, as previously shown in Figure 1.1. Building on this metaphor, we can state that the corporation is like a league of teams each with different goals and means of achieving them! A business example of a problem stemming from misalignment within an SBU would be when a marketing department creates a premium brand strategy while the production department focuses on cost cutting for a business that aims to grow substantially. The resulting misalignment may produce products that do not meet the high standards expected of the customer based on marketing and sales efforts.

Figure 1.2 depicts the bike metaphor with each function of a particular SBU representing a part of that SBU's bike. The SBUs themselves can be visualized as the bikes that are part of the larger corporate team. The important point here is that, when the corporation acts like a team, it is more likely to outperform (and beat) the competition—in this metaphor, the other corporate teams.

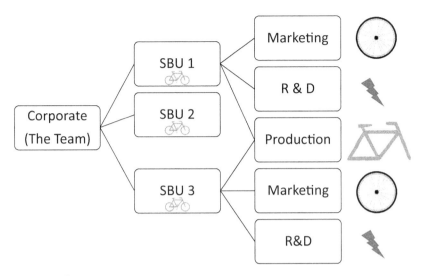

Figure 1.2 Hierarchy of strategy

Note also that the functions of each SBU can be thought of as the components for each SBU's bike. An important point that will come up later for globalized firms is that some functions can be used by one or more SBUs. In Figure 1.2 the production facilities of SBU3 are also used by SBU1. Such a structure can take advantage of the network of globalized functions by localizing some and centralizing others. We will examine this in more detail in later chapters.

The process of creating, developing and implementing a strategy for the organization is ultimately defined as "strategic management". Again, this is what this book outlines for someone interested in the strategic management of a globalized organization—an entity that intends to do something (e.g., run a business or charity) in one or more countries simultaneously.

Isn't Strategy a Plan or Something like That?

Many people associate strategy with plans. In fact, you can see the notion of a plan in the definition by Miller and Dess (1996). The problem is that many plans by themselves never constitute strategy; they remain just that: plans. Recall, the best definitions of strategy describe it as a set of decisions or actions; even Miller and Dess (1996) include decisions in theirs ... Plans by themselves are just documents. So, what's the good of plans and why/how are they related to strategy? The connection between strategy and plans is all about process versus outcome. A plan is the written outcome of the strategic management process—that of developing a strategy for your organization. So, ultimately, the main purpose of a plan is to allow you to organize thoughts on the strategy you are developing and to then communicate it to others.

General Dwight Eisenhower, who was the 34th president of the United States, referring to his philosophy on strategy, once stated: "Plans are useless. Planning is indispensable." (Note again the relationship to military strategy.) What did he mean by that? Essentially, plans are like snapshots or photos at any particular point in time. They represent the work that has already passed while developing our strategy. But recall that strategy involves a long-term process over time. Good strategy is continually updated and thus requires learning. As such, it is the learning in the process of planning your strategy that is important and not any particular codification of that process (i.e., the plan). In the military there is also the saying "Very few plans withstand contact with the enemy!". This is because the enemy is also learning and reacting to our plan. As in warfare, in business we must continually reassess how we are utilizing our resources towards our goals. When we stop and rest entirely on the initial plan, we are in a self-defeating mode.

This explains why many people become frustrated when the strategic management process becomes nothing more than an exercise to create a document that is then placed inside a drawer indefinitely. This would be an example of formulating strategy without its implementation (or, more bluntly, the "bad implementation" cell of Figure 1.1).

Emergent Strategy ("All that Happens Is Not Planned")

Emergent strategy is the concept of strategy that materializes as a "logic inherent in every major decision made within the organization"—which was not planned, but just happens! As depicted in Figure 1.3, often a strategy that is *intended* (as a plan) becomes *unrealized* and is replaced and *realized* by a strategy that *emerges* from the environment. The concept of emergent strategy was coined by the well-known strategist Henry Mintzberg (see Mintzberg & Waters, 1985). The idea is that strategy is not always "planned". The original example of such a situation was from the 1970s, when Honda attempted to enter the US market and compete against Harley Davidson. The initial plan was to sell large (high cc) motorbikes to rough *Easy Rider*–type consumers. However, as Honda salespeople attempted to implement this intended strategy, they began to realize that such a strategy might not be

Figure 1.3 Intended versus emergent strategy
Source: Adapted from Mintzberg & Waters (1985)

successful. Instead, potential buyers were more interested in the smaller cc bikes imported from Japan, and these buyers appeared to be unlike the typical biker at the time. Coupled with the actual core competence of Honda for small engine production, this led to a strategy moving away from direct competition with Harley Davidson and utilizing new and unique marketing tactics (or functional strategy), such as the "You meet the nicest people on a Honda" advertising program. The result was a successful market entry strategy very much *unlike* the original plan!

So, the question remains: Why have plans? The reasons are multifold. But to answer them we must keep in mind that plans are a *tool* for strategic management (and not strategy itself). As mentioned, plans are useful in organizing our thoughts about what our strategy will be and how we might implement it. They can be useful in communicating these ideas to a large group of people, such as shareholders or employees. But, just like any tool, they can be used for good or bad; poorly or well. The same plan that helps us coordinate our internal people may also give the competition hints as to what we believe our actions will be in future decision-making. This makes strategy a concept ripe for game theory in which we can analyze the steps and counter-steps of competitive players, much like in a game of chess. The key is that the process is continual and ongoing—making strategic management a subject that one can hardly get bored with easily … (though here we'll focus on the most important aspects of strategy we need for our purposes).

External Aspects of Strategy

For any strategy, its success will depend on how well it is linked to the external environment. That is, there are elements of the external environment that either allow or deny a strategy from happening. The environment must allow for certain actions if such actions will be useful for organizational success.

With regard to the types of strategies we are interested in—that is, either strategies typical of for-profit or not-for profit organizations—there are two levels of the external environment that are of interest. The first is the macro external environment—and, as we've learned already, "macro" means the larger environment. In particular, the macro external environment provides trends, something that is developing or changing, which may provide either an opportunity (something we can take advantage of) or threat (something which may be detrimental to our success). The key for strategic formulation is that anyone or anything in the macro environment is also exposed to these trends and may act on them. That is, our competitors and any other possible entrepreneur who may become our competitors can also see these trends and act upon them.

The other key is that these trends are usually beyond the direct control of our organization (although in many cases we may attempt to exert influence, such as when we send lobbyists to interact with politicians in an attempt to influence the political and legal environment). This is important, because it means we need to be brutally honest with ourselves about the ultimate effects of such trends. It is the recognition of these trends that helps us build an analysis of potential strategic actions, which we may, or may not, elect to implement.

The second level of the external environment is closer to the organization in terms of influence but is also not quite within its total control. (Note that control is the main concept that can distinguish between external and internal conditions. Most things beyond our control are external and those more within our control are usually internal—at least in terms of strategy and implementation.)

This second level of the environment is the industry level, and it constitutes the competitive aspects of strategy. The industry can be defined as the environment in which we compete to sell (or manage, in the case of not-for-profits) similar products and services, or "offerings". Here we are less interested in trends than in the competitive structure of the industry. However, the trends of the macro environment may in fact change the structure of the industry, which then may have effects on our competitive success.

The next chapter describes in more detail the tools and techniques used in analyzing both the macro and industrial levels of the external environment.

Internal Aspects of Strategy

Formulating successful strategy is an exercise of combining the most lucrative trends and structures of the external environment analyses with the internal capabilities and resources of the organization. That is, the internal resources and capabilities of the organization must be able to respond to the external environment for us to successfully implement a strategy based on legitimate external trends. Poor integration leads to mismatches that can result in either poor strategy (i.e., basing the logic for success on a false premise that we have the resources needed) or poor implementation (i.e., not orchestrating the resources properly). Either way, internal resources are the life-blood of an organization and must be the backbone of both strategy and its implementation for long-term success.

For example, let's say you decide that your general strategy for fame and fortune is to follow a recent trend of prime-time talent shows that play mainly to vocalists. You can't sing well but play a mean guitar. Unfortunately, this leads to a poor showing and humiliation in front of a huge TV and internet audience. In that case, you've chosen the wrong strategy! Let's say that, instead, you chose the strategy to front a band with a lead singer (that is, you've chosen to acquire a resource you did not initially have) and follow the trend of self-promotion via a video-sharing website like YouTube. Here you've done a better job of recognizing your true internal strengths and linking them well with the environment. Your strategy was good—until you broke your hand in a mountain biking tournament; so much for implementation and that old concept of (bad) luck!

We'll discuss more about how to recognize and manage the internal resources of the globalized firm towards successful strategy in Chapter 3.

How Is Strategy Related to the Globalization of the Firm?

As we've seen, strategy is important to all organizations regardless of their reasons for existing. It is also a useful concept for managing military operations, and even personal ambitions towards individual success. In fact, we've seen that strategy is a part of any set of actions that are leading towards some sense of performance—regardless of whether they are planned or not. The key is whether these actions are coherent and, like the bike team in our example earlier, leading in the same direction.

The need for a coherent logic behind an organization's strategy is even more important in cases of the globalization of the firm. Recall the normative condition. Furthermore, using a strategic approach allows us to determine the most appropriate actions that will maximize our chances of success. Explored more in Chapter 11, there are four generic strategic goals driving the decision to enter a particular foreign market. These include: (1)

(natural) resource-seeking goals, where organizations go to specific locations to access specific resources; (2) market-seeking goals, where organizations go to countries that have a high demand for their products and services; (3) efficiency-seeking goals, where organizations single out the most efficient locations featuring a combination of scale economies and low-cost factors, including agglomeration; and (4) innovation-seeking goals, where organizations target countries and regions renowned for generating world-class innovations (Peng, 2016). Knowing the logic behind the decision you are making for foreign expansion is paramount to succeeding both in choosing the correct markets/countries to enter as well as choosing the most appropriate implementation plan.

However, not all actions towards globalization have been backed up by a strong logic or strategy. The initial entry of many foreign firms into China after it opened up some of its markets in the late 1970s resulted in a lot of hemorrhaging of cash and, eventually, big losses. The main strategy for some seemed to be "If I don't get in there now my competitors will and they'll beat me to the punch!". Unfortunately, that is similar to the action of jumping off a building because your friend did: usually not recommended—but if you do, make sure you have a parachute for low altitudes! The result in China was a lot of unsuccessful bids and exits by the newcomers. Later, during the early 2000s, as the environment became more business-friendly and companies had a better understanding of how to do business in China, the success rates and profitability of foreign entities in China improved. One major difference was the ability to be more strategic in the market entry for later newcomers. Of course, much of this had to do with more and better information about the business environment. Initially entry was marked by high uncertainty but the promise of great reward. The "more than one billion plus" population seemed at the time to be too large to ignore. However, even today the average annual disposable income in China is only 12,932 yuan (or about US$1,913) (China Daily, 2017). In 1978 it was 343.40 yuan (or less than US$50) per year! Such a market may be large but hardly sustaining for most Western businesses.

Ultimately, the lesson is that the strategist needs to carefully analyze the options for the organization in order to maximize the potential for success. This book is structured to do that for any organization building upon a globalized strategy. Each chapter helps guide you towards developing a better understanding of the organization and its global environment, with the aim of determining the appropriate strategy and its implementation with regard to managing the globalized organization.

References

Ansoff, H. I. (1979). *Strategic management*. London: Macmillan.

Barnard, C. I. (1938). *The functions of the executive*. Boston: Harvard University Press.

Barney, J. (2001). Resource-based theories of competitive advantage: A ten-year retrospective on the resource-based view. *Journal of Management, 27*(1), 643–650.

Chandler, A. (1962). *Strategy and structure: Chapters in the history of the American industrial enterprise*. Cambridge: MIT Press.

China Daily (2017). China's per capita disposable income up 8.8% in H1. July 17. Retrieved from www.chinadaily.com.cn/business/2017-07/17/content_30140898.htm (last accessed August 6, 2018).

Drucker, P. F. (1954). *The practice of management*. New York: Harper & Brothers.

Hambrick, D. (1980). Operationalizing the concept of business-level strategy in research. *Academy of Management Review, 5*(1), 567–575.

Miller, D., & Dess, G. (1996). *Strategic management* (2nd ed.). New York: McGraw Hill.

Mintzberg, H. (1979). *The structuring of organizations*. Englewood Cliffs, NJ: Prentice-Hall.

Mintzberg, H., & Waters, J. A. (1985). Of strategies, deliberate and emergent. *Strategic Management, 6*(3), 257–272.

Peng, M. (2016). *GLOBAL3*. New York: Cengage Learning.

Porter, M. E. (1980). *Competitive strategy: Techniques for analyzing industries and competitors*. New York: Free Press.

Porter, M. (1996). What is strategy? *Harvard Business Review, 74*(6), 61–78.

Rumelt, R. P., Schendel, D. E., & Teece, D. J. (1994). Fundamental issues in strategy. In Rumelt, R. P., Schendel, D. E., & Teece, D. J. (Eds.). *Fundamental issues in strategy: A research agenda* (pp. 9–47). Boston: Harvard Business School Press.

Von Neumann, J., & Morgenstern, O. (1947). *Theory of games and economic behavior* (2nd rev. ed.). Princeton: Princeton University Press.

Techniques for Analyzing the External Environment

2

Learning Objectives

By the end of this chapter, you will:

- Understand the six main components of the external environment imbedded in the PESTEL framework;
- Comprehend how each PESTEL component may influence the strategic analysis for a globalized organization;
- Know the five elements of the industry-level analysis called the "five forces" model;
- Understand the addition of a sixth industrial "force";
- Comprehend how each "five forces" component may influence the strategic analysis for a globalized organization;
- Know the "double diamond" model of national advantage at the industry level.

Practice Objectives

By the end of this chapter, you will be able to:

- Define the elements of the PESTEL framework;
- Analyze and create a PESTEL analysis for any country in the world;
- Define the elements of the five forces framework;
- Analyze and create a five forces analysis for any industry in the world;

- Analyze and create a double diamond model analysis for an industry in a particular country of the world:
- Create an external factor evaluation (EFE) analysis.

PESTEL Model of the External Macro Environment

Recall from Chapter 1 that elements of the external environment are important for creating and implementing strategic actions that may increase the effectiveness of any strategy chosen by the organization. Thus, it would be useful to have a way to categorize and analyze the elements of the external environment that are likely to affect the success of the organization itself. The PESTEL framework is one useful categorization of the external environment's major elements, which every organization should actively survey for creating and updating its strategy. PESTEL is an acronym created from the first letters of each major environmental component, namely political, economic, social, technological, environmental and legal. (There are other frameworks that may be useful for a particular industry or situation but PESTEL is a good general one to use. The key is to be exhaustive enough in the analysis to minimize missing an important trend while avoiding over-analysis and wasted effort and / or analysis paralysis, whereby too much unfiltered information leads to inaction.)

Let's take a look at each component individually and see how it affects our potential strategy. While looking at these components keep in mind what was mentioned in Chapter 1: That these are best thought of as trends or existing institutions that may have a material effect on the success of the organization but that the organization cannot control itself.

Political

Political factors consist of aspects of the macro environment that are related to governmental institutions. For the globalized firm, these usually equate to the political systems of the countries that the organization is either operating within or thinking about entering. In terms of business, and even the organization of people for a not-for-profit, norms towards "freedom of association" and the "right to organize" may affect the ability to form an organization within a country. (We'll see later that the political norms and attitudes often relate to the legal factors, too. In fact, all are ultimately interrelated in many ways.)

A general breakdown of political stances can be made into democratic and non-democratic norms, with the former being defined as allowing for the freely elected representatives of the people and the latter involving dictatorships and one-party systems of government. As PESTEL is all about trends—essentially, the general direction of environmental changes—we can look for whether political changes are favorable or unfavorable for our organization. (As we'll see, the former are opportunities and the latter threats.) A general trend discernible at the beginning of the 2020s has been towards authoritarian, right-wing governments.

Economic

Economic factors, in general, consist of the aspects relevant to the allocation of resources within a society. These will relate back to political factors, in that certain political systems are more inclined towards certain economic organizations. For example, capitalism, in which the means of production are owned by private citizens via capital markets, is often associated with democratic politics. State ownership is usually, but not always, associated with communistic or socialistic politics. But note that these are two poles in a diametrically opposed spectrum— and that explains why we must separate out the political from the economic when analyzing the general macro environment. Why? The reason is because most countries consist of varying degrees of ownership rights and citizens' rights. For example, although China has been considered a communist country since the middle of the twentieth century, it has actually moved radically in terms of its economic institutions, while remaining steadfast in its system of one-party rule. Thus, while China can be seen economically as having somewhat free markets (while still dominated by state-owned businesses), its political system is still monolithic with regard to the Communist Party of China. This type of polity creates interesting dichotomies in how to do business in countries that have such eclectic mixes of economic and political policies. For China, it has meant that money can be made by foreign investors due to open markets but at the political (potential) risk of expropriation of the company's assets if, and when, the Communist Party decides to "stop the party" …

The system of allocating resources ultimately results in measures of economic health that you can utilize while analyzing whether the country makes sense for your organization's strategy. Thus, metrics like gross domestic product (GDP) or average income or wages per capita may work into the analysis. For example, if you are trying to sell within a country you will want to ensure that wages are high enough to buy your products. If you want to produce your product in a country you will be interested in wages, but for a different reason: You may want to ensure that wages are low enough to remain competitive worldwide. Recall, strategy as the "logic that links things together" applies here. The importance of environmental trends will depend on what your initial goals are and other things, such as the nature of the industry.

Social

Social factors have to do with the general milieu of the greater environment—that is, the important trends that are changing the ways people think and feel and what people are doing more, or less, of in their daily lives. Social factors often take the form of fashions or trends, like the health food fad when people try to eat more healthily. Trends are particularly important for developing business strategy because they are often based on what people, in general, value, and therefore can provide ample opportunities to exploit, such as, in the health food case, the opportunity to sell organic foods.

Each category of environmental factors is interrelated and can also be combined to create more specific categories for analysis. For example, socio-economic factors are a combination of social and economic elements. They can be extremely useful in analyzing potential for opportunities development. For example, something like the prominence of a middle class in a particular country may help determine whether the population can sustain a certain type of business.

Technological

Technology is pervasive today, and technological trends can also provide for business opportunities. Technological factors refer to the tools and techniques utilized in getting work done by individuals and organizations. Essentially, a technology is a tool for productivity—like robotics in manufacturing, software in computing or the internet in communications. We may be interested in selling such tools or utilizing them in our organization. Either way, the trends in the external environment will be important barometers in knowing what the environment can manage in terms of technological utilization.

Technology may also be an important element for deciding whether to enter a new market or not and how to enter—or if deciding to enter after all. Questions of whether the market can sustain a technology or can be supported by a technology need to be asked. For example, when computer company Dell first decided to enter China it needed to change its traditional online sales approach and open retail stores. At the time the Chinese market for computers was new, and many Chinese consumers would not use credit cards to purchase goods over the internet.

Technological standards differ throughout the world and must be a part of any analysis for market entry as well. For example, codes used for mobile phones differ across the world. Electrical outlets and the voltage output of those outlets also differ across countries. Standards and infrastructure will make a difference. Interestingly, the first innovations in mobile banking did not come from the West but from Kenya, where the lack of telephone landline infrastructure and brick-and-mortar bank branches accelerated the adoption of such technology as M-PESA.

Environmental

The "environment" here refers to the ecosystem in which your organization is embedded. The way we treat the ecosystem changes over time and across countries, but in general trends towards more sustainable business practices have evolved. This makes sense if we want our organizations to continue to survive over time. Depleting non-renewable resources for which our organization is dependent, for instance, means that it is only a matter of time before we run out of business!

Another major environmental trend is related to climate change. Regardless of whether the climate change is man-made, data shows that the world in general is getting hotter and individual weather patterns more erratic. This has had a real effect on various parts of the world. For example, forest fires and hurricanes are increasing in number and intensity; world water levels are rising due to melting of the polar caps. These events generate both opportunities and threats for various businesses and organizations. Knowing how climate change is affecting various countries and regions can help one determine these opportunities and threats and then develop strategies to meet them.

Legal

These factors are related to political factors discussed earlier (and may be related to other factors, such as social trends) but we separate them out for a more nuanced understanding of the general environment. Legal factors specifically refer to the laws and regulations of the environment being studied. Legal aspects are particularly salient for managing an organization without getting into trouble with authorities and properly managing within the institutional setting. The details of the legal systems and frameworks of any particular country or region may be specific for any particular industry or practices, and knowledge of these legal issues is paramount. For example, strong regulations related to car exhausts and fuel efficiencies in California, an economy larger than many countries, means that car companies that wish to sell cars in the state must adhere to strict environmental standards. This has had a powerful impact on car designs outside California itself.

Analyzing a Country's External Environmental Sphere Using the PESTEL Approach

It is helpful to use the PESTEL categories and apply them to specific regions and countries while generating an analysis of the trends. Doing this provides a useful list of potential opportunities and threats presented in that environment, which we utilize later in the book.

Five Forces Model of the External Industrial Environment

A major aspect of the external environment for any organization is the industry in which it is embedded. This includes both for-profit and not-for-profit organizations. Industry is usually defined as the collection of all the organizations offering similar products or services. To include all types of circumstances, whether products or services, we will call these "offerings".

Industry is important, because it determines the boundaries and constraints by which any activities can be done. This results in the notion of competitiveness, with highly competitive industries, like pizza shops, resulting in less profit for the owners and less competitive industries, like pharmaceuticals, resulting in high profits. In fact, some research suggests that the industry context can explain up to 20 percent of profits of for-profit firms.

But what is meant by industry competitiveness and why is high competitiveness linked to low profits? Isn't competition a good thing in business? The answer—like all things strategic—requires us to be precise and organized in our thinking. Competition is good for the general public because it allows for the most efficient flow of resources. Consumers like competition! It usually leads to lower prices and more choice in products and services. But, for companies to be more profitable, some of that efficiency must be absorbed and kept by the company rather than given to consumers in the form of price reductions and new and better products. Originally, the study of monopolies and oligopolies, which were forms of industrial structures that led to very low competitiveness, was done by industrial organization (IO) economists. The IO economists, in general, argued against monopolies because of the lack of consumer surplus and ongoing efficient flow of resources, as well as the concentration of wealth that resulted. The problem is that under such systems innovation and overall economic growth may be constrained.

Some argue that the IO perspective was anti-business, because it argued against the unconstrained growth in any one business' activities—that is, the creation of monopolies and the surplus profit that results. The problem is that this is often one of the major goals of any for-profit firm—i.e., to increase profits and growth. The famous and prolific strategist Michael Porter, who will be mentioned a few times in this book, essentially flipped IO economics on its end in his seminal book, entitled *Competitive Strategy* (Porter, 1980). In developing the five forces model he, essentially, depicts the elements of the industrial structure that help to reinforce a monopolistic position. In other words, one way to look at the five forces is to ask yourself: Does the aspect, or force, of the environment create or exert a monopolistic effect or not? Another question to ask is: How attractive is this industry to you as a potential outside investor? Note that highly competitive industries will be less attractive because, in cases of higher competitiveness, much of the potential profits available will be "given" to consumers (buyers) or other industry players. So, when we say an industry is highly competitive, we also mean that it is not attractive for investment.

We will examine each force now using this perspective. This is particularly advantageous when thinking about industrial structure from a global perspective. We can combine the macroeconomic analysis of any particular country with the five forces for the industry within that country, because some countries' contexts may or may not support monopolistic tendencies and thus reinforce or deplete the power of the industrial force.

The five forces model (Porter, 2008) is illustrated in Figure 2.1 (complements, or complementors, mentioned soon, are an added sixth force). It is often depicted as including a supply chain link, shown horizontally linking suppliers with the industry players and then buyers. Being precise and clear is important in defining members of each group. Using the definition of industry, rivals are competitors that present similar offerings. They constitute players currently within the industry. Although your organization will be in

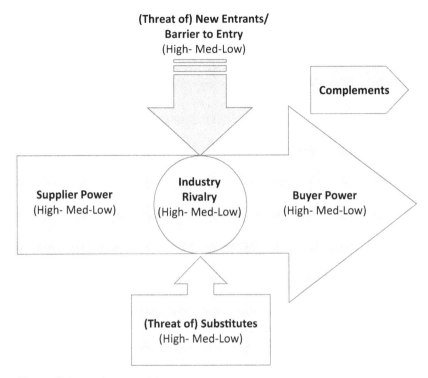

Figure 2.1 Five forces model
Sources: Adapted from Porter (1980, 2008); Brandenburger & Nalebuff (1996)

the group of rivals, we need to be careful to do the analysis from the industry, and not firm, level. To some extent, all players in the industry are affected similarly by these industrial forces. Thus, this five forces model explains *industry-level* competitiveness and attractiveness. (We talk more about the individual organization's competitiveness *at the firm level* in the next chapter.) Overall, each of the forces must be analyzed and the whole work combined for a holistic analysis of the industry's attractiveness. It is the overall picture of industry attractiveness and not any single force that is important.

"Suppliers" are players outside the "core" or focal industry who sell offerings that are inputs to the industry's offerings. Buyers are players outside the focal industry who buy the industry's offerings. "(Threat of) new entrants" covers players outside the industry who may become rivals in the future. (Note that I include "threat of" within brackets because new entrants may or may not exist to create the force's effect—i.e., the mere threat of a new player entering the industry may be enough to affect the monopolistic tendencies of that industry …) These potential new entrants may include suppliers or buyers as well as players unrelated to the industry. "(Threat of) substitutes" covers offerings from outside the industry that may be used as substitutes for the industry's offerings. Note the importance of being outside the industry; offerings within the industry are competitive offerings and are categorized under the "Industry rivalry" force. Potential substitutes may or may not become competitive offerings but it is their "potentiality" or possibility of becoming competitive offerings that exerts a monopolistic tendency for an industry.

A sixth force was argued to influence the tendency towards monopolistic effects, called "Complements" or "Complementors" (note that this is spelled with an "e" and not an "i"). Complementors are offerings from outside the industry that may benefit the industry's offerings by enhancing the positive attractiveness of the industry's offerings when complements are included (Brandenburger & Nalebuff, 1996).

Let's look at each of these forces individually.

Industry Rivalry (of Competitors)

One of the most important aspects of competitors is how many there are and of what size. Thus, while analyzing the rivalry in an industry, we often start with measuring the industry concentration. Industry concentration measures the number and size of competitors within the industry. The more competitors and the smaller their own market share, the more competitive (and less attractive) an industry will be. Recall that we can use the tendency towards monopolistic structures as a proxy of the competitiveness. The least competitive industry would be a monopoly with one player with 100 percent market share. As the industry increases in rival players and their individual market shares go down, competition increases. But concentration of market share can affect the actual competitive effects of rivalry. The easiest measure to use is called C4, which is defined as the combined market share of the top four industry players. (You may also use C8 or C10, etc., as measures.) Thus, the industry may have 100 players, but if the top four organizations have 80 percent of the entire market such an oligopoly (i.e., small number of powerful players) may still provide a less competitive industry (though the 96 other players are likely to be less competitive themselves).

The Herfindahl–Hirschman index (HHI) is another common measure of market concentration, which allows for more subtle effects, though it is more complex than C4 or C8 measures and requires the share of all industry firms. In fact, it is used by the US Department of Justice to determine whether to allow mergers within an industry. Mergers that increase the HHI by more than 200 points may raise antitrust concerns. The HHI is calculated by squaring the market share of each firm in the industry and summing the results for the industry as such:

$HHI = F1^2 + F2^2 + F3^2 + ... + Fn^2$ (where F is the market share of each firm rounded to a whole number)

HHIs of less than 1,500 are competitive industries; HHIs of 1,500 to 2,500 are moderately concentrated and less competitive industries; and HHIs of 2,500 or greater are considered highly concentrated, non-competitive industries.

Other aspects that may affect the attractiveness of an industry via rivalry can be seen under the "Industry rivalry" section of Figure 2.1. Exit barriers are costs associated with leaving an industry, like selling off capital equipment and inventory. Obviously, higher exit costs mean some competitors will tough it out even as competition increases, making the industry potentially even more competitive. Fixed costs, overcapacity and corporate stakes are similar costs that may affect competition.

Industries that are growing allow for more room in competition and pricing compared to those that are stagnant or shrinking. Thus, high-growth industries may be less competitive (and usually more attractive) than low-growth industries.

Finally, aspects of organizational differentiation may affect the degree of rivalry within an industry. We look more closely at how this may be done in the next chapter, on the internal environment of the organization. From the perspective of the industry and the five forces model, industry attractiveness may increase if the industry allows for more diversity in offerings and switching costs (associated with moving from one competitor's offerings to anothers) are high. Diversity of rivals and brand identity are important differentiation factors.

As with all the forces in the five forces model, a balance is maintained from the interactions of various elements or aspects of each force. Thus, the elements are evaluated and their interactions assessed to obtain an overall score for the force in terms of its effects on industry attractiveness. We often depict each force as low, medium or high in terms of its effects such that, if rivalry is deemed "high", then the effect on industry attractiveness is negative (while a low-rivalry industry would be positive).

Some of these elements or aspects of competitive rivalry that you should evaluate are:

- Concentration (of market share)
- Exit barriers
- Fixed costs and valued added for industry
- Industry growth
- Industry capacity (overcapacity)
- Product differentiation
- Switching costs between competitors
- Brand identity
- Rival diversity
- Importance of the business unit to the larger corporation that owns it

Power of Suppliers

Suppliers sell their offerings to the focal industry players. In determining the monopolistic effects that influence the attractiveness (or ability of the industry to generate super-normal profits), the concept of (bargaining) power is important. Power is the ability of one player to coerce another player to do its bidding. Simply put, powerful suppliers can better dictate the price they charge for their offerings and more easily squeeze the profits of core industry players.

Just like industry rivalry, concentration of suppliers will affect the competitive dynamic. In general, the more concentrated the suppliers are, the more power they will have to dictate pricing. Imagine, for example, only one supplier exists. To the supplier, it is a monopoly (single seller), and, all else being equal, can charge maximum prices and obtain the entire consumer surplus available. A small number of suppliers represent an oligopoly with fairly high power for the suppliers. As concentration decreases and supplier rivalry increases, the power of suppliers to bargain with industry players decreases.

Factors that may mitigate even a monopoly situation include the presence of substitute inputs, the threat of backwards integration and the supply cost relative to the total cost of industry inputs. That is, if the core industry players can threaten to become competitors to the industry monopolist, they can force the monopolist to bring prices down at least enough to mitigate such integration. The importance of volume to the supplier in creating economies of scale may also play a role in bargaining power. If a certain minimum efficiency scale exists where a company needs to produce a certain number of units to make a profit, the pressure towards concentration increases. The importance of a specific offering for the differentiation of the core industry players will affect power as well as the switching costs associated with going from one supplier to another. In cases like this, the harder it is to find an alternative supplier, the greater the power of the supplier.

Some aspects of "Supplier power" that you should evaluate are:

- Concentration (of suppliers)
- Economies of scale for suppliers (volume)
- Value/impact of inputs towards costs and differentiation
- Switching costs (of changing suppliers)
- Existence of input substitutes
- Threat of forward integration
- Costs relative to total purchases for industry

Power of Buyers

Buyers are on the other side of the coin to suppliers in the relationship with focal industry players. Like suppliers, powerful buyers can better dictate the price they pay for their offerings and more easily squeeze the profits of core industry players. Depending on where the industry players lie in the supply chain/network of the industry, the buyers may be other organizations that use the focal industry offerings as input into their own offerings or the buyers may be end users of the offerings (as in the final "consumers").

Again, concentration, especially vis-à-vis the industry, is important. A single buyer is called a monopsony and, like its cousin, the monopoly, often holds a powerful bargaining position. This has an even stronger effect when there are many "sellers" or rivals in the focal industry.

A number of characteristics of the buyer can affect its bargaining power. If the buyer is purchasing a lot of its inputs from the industry it may or may not provide more power, depending on such factors as possible substitute offerings and product differentiation. Buying a lot from a supplier might give the buyer more power as a volume purchaser but if the supplier is itself a monopolist it may force the buyer to share the excess profits or cut off supply. Thus, the actual power of players in the five forces model will depend on subtle "gives and takes", often predicated on the control of various resources necessary for producing the offerings within the supply chain/network.

Some aspects of "Buyer power" that you should evaluate are:

- Concentration (of buyers versus industry)
- Volume (of purchases)
- Information asymmetry (of buyers to sellers)
- Brand identity (of industry products/services)
- Price sensitivity (of buyers)
- Differentiation (of industry products/services)
- Buyer incentives offered
- Threat of backwards integration
- Availability of substitutes

(Threat of) New Entrants

As mentioned earlier, new entrants are competitors that are new to the industry. The threat of new entrants is the potentiality that new entrants *might* enter the industry. Thus, what is important is the likelihood that new entrants can successfully become competitors. This is pertinent because a new entrant increases the number of rivals and lowers market concentration, so that, in general, new entrants to the industry increase competition and, thus, decrease the industry's attractiveness (for existing players).

Usually, when analyzing the threat of new entrants, we examine the existing barriers to entry. That is, what factors exist that might increase the costs of entering the industry? Many of these barriers are economically based. For example, economies of scale may create a minimum efficiency scale, which means that a certain capacity of production is most efficient for a single player or industry. Entry of a new player would create overcapacity and lower the profits of all players—including the entrant—thereby deterring any outside player from even contemplating entry. Adding factors such as learning curves that are based on cumulative production gives advantages to existing players and adds costs to potential new entrants. Such situations make potential industry investments less attractive.

Other factors such as capital requirements, brand identity and switching costs may give the incumbent players an advantage and deter new entrants. Government policies either for or against industry concentration will affect the quality of barriers to entry for new entrants.

In general, the higher barriers are, and thus the costs of entering, the more attractive the industry is to existing players. However, the dynamics of other factors, again, need to be taken into account. Depending on the effects of other factors, it may be worthwhile for a potential entrant to enter the market even in the face of high entry barriers. After all, the industry is actually an attractive investment when it has high barriers to entry. The key is whether the potential entrant has other characteristics that allow it to withstand the cost pressures of entry. For example, the proprietary pharmaceutics industry has many high barriers, including government policy (directed in the United States by the Food and Drug Administration) and high research and marketing costs. However, once a company creates a patentable drug it can reap extraordinary profits; in part, this can be explained by taking all the five forces into account. Overcoming these barriers will also require development of internal resources and assets, which are discussed in Chapter 3.

Some aspects of "(Threat of) new entrants" that you should evaluate are:

- Cost advantages (of incumbents)
- Capital requirements for initial entry
- Proprietary learning curves
- Access to inputs
- Government policies (on firm size, input access, etc.)
- Economies of scale
- Brand identity
- Switching costs
- Access to complimentary assets (such as distribution, labor markets, etc.)
- Intellectual and other legal protections of proprietary products
- Expectations of retaliation

(Threat of) Substitutes

The greater the availability of substitute offerings from other industries and the easier and less costly it is to switch; the more competitive pressures are put on the focal industry itself. It is important to point out and emphasize that substitute offerings, like new entrants, are not competitive offerings within the industry context. They represent potential threats based on their *potentiality* to become a threat to industry attractiveness. That is, they do not represent direct competition, like the offerings of the industry rivals. However, this does not mean that they do not exert, currently at the time of one's analysis or in the future, an existential threat to the industry's profitability or attractiveness. Nor does it mean that the substitute offering may not one day become a competitor's offering.

A good example of this is seen in the offerings of the soft drink industry. Years ago it might have been possible to discuss the soft drink and bottled water markets as distinct industries. Coke and Pepsi were direct competitors in the soft drink industry and Pellegrino and Evian were bottled water competitors. However, water and soda pop were then substitute offerings. Both could satiate thirst (at least for a while) but did not directly compete with each other, particularly because the bottled water offerings at the time were expensive and distinct enough to be separated as "industries". The external trend towards healthier sources of hydration and the success of brands like Evian and the competitive threat of these substitutes eventually led Coke and Pepsi towards investing in bottled water and driving prices down. Today, what was the substitute offering of bottled water has become a competitive offering within the industry dominated by the two soft drink companies, owners of the Coke and Pepsi brands. This makes even more sense when one considers that water represents an upstream resource in the value chain of the original "soft drink" industry.

Some aspects of "(Threat of) substitutes" that you should evaluate are:

- Switching costs (towards substitutes)
- Price–performance tradeoffs (of substitutes)
- Variety and number (of substitutes)
- Necessity of industry products/services
- Brand identity
- Buyer inclination towards substitutes

(Benefits of) Complementors

Complements are offerings from outside the industry that may benefit the industry's offerings by enhancing their positive attractiveness. A good example is applications software, or "apps", which can be defined as a separate industry from the hardware used to run the apps, like computers or smartphones. A smartphone without apps is not much use, so the software offerings help to complement the hardware of the smartphone industry. The more complements that are available, the more attractive the industry (and, by straight logic, the less competitive). Complementors are the organizations that offer the complements. Complementors help to boost the attractiveness of each industry.

The soft drink industry example above can also be used to illustrate the use of complementors in driving strategic directions. In the case of water, we saw a substitute become a competitive offering and, essentially, a part of the industry's offerings. Snacks and junk food, interesting the opposite of the health trend that drove bottled water forward, represent complement offerings to those in the soft drink industry. However, the notion of co-opetition becomes apparent with complementors. That is, complementors may wish to work with each other due to the positive associations but may also become competitors at some point. This led companies like PepsiCo in the soft drink industry to diversify into junk food brands like Cheetos such that complementors became competitors.

Some aspects of "Complements" that you should evaluate are:

- Variety and number (of complements)
- Relative value added
- Barriers to entry (of complements)
- Difficulty of engaging complements
- Buyer perception of complements
- Exclusivity of complement

Analyzing a Country's Industrial Structure Using the Five Forces and Double Diamond Approaches

The five forces model can be used to analyze the industry within any particular country. However, giving the global nature of business, the country industry is likely to also be characterized by the global industry. Recall that it is important to define upfront what the boundaries for your industry will be. The concepts from the five forces model, of substitutes and complementors, make this clear. For example, we might define our industry narrowly as the carbonated water or soft drink industry, in which case snacks like potato chips would be considered complementors and our competitors seen narrowly as other soft drink producers. However, we may also wish to expand our industry definition to include fast foods (or some other category), in which case we bring inward the offerings that in the first example were outside the industry. The choice is up to the analyst and will depend on where the competitive threats already seem to exist.

Michael Porter, who introduced the five forces, also created a model called the "double diamond" in order to explain the determinants of national advantage at the industry level (Porter, 1990). In other words, some industries are naturally suited to some countries. As you can see in Figure 2.2, the five forces can help explain the category of industry structure, listed as "Firm strategy

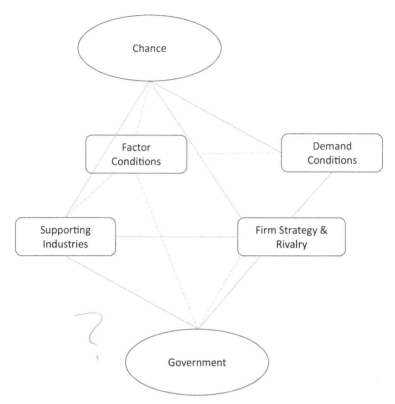

Figure 2.2 General double diamond model

Source: Adapted from Porter (1990)

and rivalry". "Factor conditions" are things like raw materials, which could be minerals or other higher-end inputs, such as human capital (i.e., an educated workforce). "Demand conditions" are things like high GDP and spending per capita. "Supporting industries" are those that are part of the value chain/network for the focal industry.

We have seen the aspect of "Chance", depicted in Figure 2.2, as the concept of luck presented in Chapter 1. The aspect of "Government" alludes to the policies and actions of a country's political actors to help nurture (or destroy) an industry within its national boundaries. An example of a country that, by chance, was ideal for the formation of an oil industry is the United Arab Emirates (UAE), which before oil reserves were discovered was, essentially, a desert populated by nomadic tribes whose main industry was pearl harvesting. Demand conditions, at least early on, like factor conditions, came from outside the country, via the support of American interests. Support industries, like refineries, were initially based outside. Government polices helped develop the industry further, and, based on the exploitation of its oil resources, the UAE became a very rich country. However, knowing that the oil reserves are non-renewable resources, the country's leadership (based on a monarchy) has invested in other industrial opportunities, such as renewable energy sources and tourism in the city of Dubai, for example (which has an indoor ski slope in a country where the outside temperature regularly reaches 100° Fahrenheit!). Thus, the effects of government policy help to extend upon the industry structure effects.

Researching and analyzing the conditions of the double diamond for any country you are interested in investigating will help determine whether the industry in that country is viable or not. Thus, you can use it to analyze the potential for your industry in that country.

Creating an External Factor Evaluation (EFE) Analysis

Now that we know a number of external analysis tools we can create an evaluation of potential opportunities and threats that may affect industry players. We can prepare an evaluation of how well the current strategy allows the SBU to take advantage of opportunities and to avoid or rework threats by developing an EFE analysis and its associated matrix table.

To do this, start by listing all the factors identified as trends from your PESTEL and industry analyses. You can narrow down the assignment by choosing the top ten of each positive or negative trend (i.e., opportunity or threat) to industry players. (Note that these are trends that are happening in the environment, whether macro or industrial, to which all industry players are exposed.) Careful wording is recommended; often use of a noun expression followed by "is increasing" or "is decreasing" helps to create clarity. Remember: Trends are changes in a macro environment factor/element that is either going up or down.

Once the top list is selected, assign a weight of importance to each trend. The weight should represent the relative importance of the factor to the success of the SBU under review. The total of the weights should equal 1.0.

Finally, you should rate each factor as to how effective the current strategy is with respect to taking advantage of the opportunities and avoiding the threats. The scale is 1 to 4, with 4 being very effective at taking advantage of opportunities and avoiding threats. Multiply the weights by the ratings and sum the resulting scores.

Table 2.1 External factor evaluation

OPPORTUNITIES	Description	Weight	Rating	Score
1	Foreign interest in industry offerings is growing	0.15	2	0.3
2	population to warm weather areas is shifting	0.2	3	0.6
3	Skilled labor pool of aging population is increasing	0.1	1	0.1
4	Availability of support technology is increasing	0.1	4	0.4
5, etc.	Markets for our offerings are growing	0.05	3	0.15
THREATS				
1	Client demographic is aging	0.05	1	0.05
2	Industry rivalry is increasing	0.2	2	0.4
3	Inflation is increasing	0.05	3	0.15
4, etc.	Supplier power is increasing	0.1	2	0.2
		1		2.35

Table 2.1 depicts an example of an EFE matrix table with four to five items per trend type. Note that the final weighted score of 2.35 is slightly below the natural weighted average of 2.50 (i.e., $(1 + 4) / 2 = 2.5$). This is an indication that the current strategy is doing slightly lower than average in taking advantage of opportunities and avoiding threats.

References

Brandenburger, A. M., & Nalebuff, B. J. (1996). *Co-opetition*. New York: Currency Doubleday.

Porter, M. E. (1980). *Competitive strategy: Techniques for analyzing industries and competitors*. New York: Free Press

Porter, M. E. (1990). *The competitive advantage of nations*. New York: Free Press.

Porter, M. E. (2008). The five competitive forces that shape strategy. *Harvard Business Review*, 86(1), 78–93.

Techniques for Analyzing the Internal Environment

3

Learning Objectives

By the end of this chapter, you will:

- Understand what is meant by the resource-based view (RBV) of the organization;
- Comprehend the notions of resources (and assets) and capabilities as well as the concept of a core competence of an organization;
- Know the seven categories of resources from the resource advantage (RA) theory framework;
- Understand the meaning of the value–rarity–imitability–organization (VRIO) model and the RBV perspective on strategic competitive advantage;
- Comprehend how resources and capabilities may influence the strategic analysis for a globalized organization.

Practice Objectives

By the end of this chapter, you will be able to:

- Categorize the seven types of resources for a particular organization;
- Identify the core competence of a particular organization;
- Analyze any assets, capabilities and competences using the VRIO model;
- Create an internal factor evaluation (IFE) analysis of a particular organization.

The RBV Perspective on Strategy

The previous chapter discussed at length the structural determinants of profitability for any particular industry and, thus, any organization within the industry. As noted, 20 percent of the profit for for-profit firms is explained by industry structure using, for example, the five forces model. However, the question persists of what might explain the other 80 percent! The answer—as argued in scholarly works on strategy, like Wernerfelt (1984), Barney (1991) and Hunt and Morgan (1995)—lies in the internal strengths of the organizations themselves.

The RBV perspective on strategy developed in order to describe from where the strengths of an organization came and helped to differentiate between successful and less successful competitors within the same industry. Thus, the RBV perspective attempted to answer questions like: Why did Walmart do so well competing against Kmart? What were the fundamental forces underlying the strengths that the former company had over the latter?

The key, it was argued, was the resources that successful companies had that less successful ones did not, as well as the way in which those companies deployed and utilized these important resources.

Resources (Assets), Capabilities and Core Competences

Resources, in general, can be categorized into the assets (both tangible and intangible) and the capabilities of which the organization has some ownership and control. As such, these are internal factors, and hence the topic of this chapter as the internal environment (of the organization). Note the importance of control, as alluded to in the last chapter. Internal assets (e.g., employees) may not be "owned" per se but they can to some extent be "controlled"—or perhaps it is better expressed as "influenced"—in ways external actors cannot. This is a major important differentiator between internal and external strategic actors.

In the literature, resources are often synonymous with the term "assets", but they can also represent all aspects of internal strengths—like capabilities—so here I refer to the general concept of internal strengths as "resources" and specific items that give the organization its strength as "assets". That is, resources incorporate assets, capabilities and, as we'll see, higher-ordered competences.

Table 3.1 Seven categories of resources

Resource	Description/example
Financial	• Cash reserves and access to financial markets
Physical	• Plant, raw material and equipment
Legal	• Trademarks and licensees
Human	• Skills and knowledge of individual employees, including, importantly, their entrepreneurial skills
Relational	• Relationships between competitors, suppliers and customers
Organizational	• Controls, routines, cultures, competences including, importantly, a competence for entrepreneurship
Informational	• Knowledge about market segments, competitors and technology

Sources: Hunt (2000); Hunt & Morgan (1995)

Hunt (2000) defines resources as the tangible and intangible entities available to firms that enable them to produce market offerings that have value for some market segment(s). He categorizes resources into seven distinct categories, as depicted in Table 3.1.

The resources illustrated in Table 3.1 include all types, both tangible and intangible, as well as capabilities—but separating these out can be instructive. For example, describing assets in terms of tangibility is important, because the less tangible an asset or resource is, the more likely it will provide protection against imitation. This, as we will see, is one aspect towards determining the importance of a resource for strategic purposes. Tangible assets are "things" that can be touched and seen (although sometimes that might not be easy as in the example of capital resources, which are held in a bank deposit but could be eventually "grabbed" in the form of actual cash). Intangible assets are invisible to the eye and are more conceptual, but in many cases are even more important for competitive advantage. Often, tangible expressions of an intangible asset also exist, such as in the case of patent drawings. However, in the case of a patent, the asset itself is not the piece of paper describing the patented technology but actually a legal apparatus, and it gets its value from the ability of the courts to protect the patent's use and enforce judgment.

Table 3.2 shows general examples of each category of tangible and intangible assets for many organizations.

Capabilities are specific resources that refer to the important skills at which the organization is adept. That is, they are things that the organization can do (not things that they own—i.e., assets), which may be of value to the strategic goals of the organization. While some are more identifiable than others, capabilities as skills tend to be intangible. They are embedded in the routines and procedures of the organization—such as logistics skills or sales skills.

Table 3.2 Examples of tangible and intangible assets

Tangible	Intangible
Labor	Reputation and brand equity
Capital	Proprietary knowledge
	(trade secrets, R&D discoveries)
Buildings/plant	Culture and organizational abilities
Land	Intellectual properties
	(patents, designs, trademarks, copyrights)
Equipment and materials	

Note: R&D = research and development.

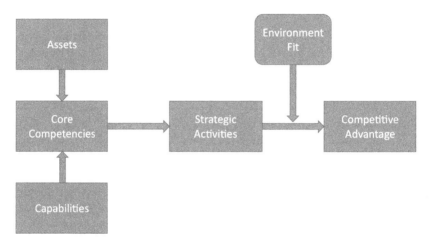

Figure 3.1 Relationship of assets and capabilities to core competence in creating strategic competitive advantage

Source: Adapted from Barney (1991)

As illustrated in Figure 3.1, core competences are higher-level manifestations of the enactment of a combination of an organization's assets and capabilities. Core competences reinforce the activities that the organization enacts that give it competitive advantage and lead to successful strategic goal achievement. We saw an example of this earlier in the book with the example of the core competence that underlay the emergent strategy of Honda's North American market entry in the 1970s—namely Honda's competence in designing, manufacturing and marketing small engines. This led to Honda focusing on activities that leverage this core competence, which in turn is supported by the assets and capabilities in which Honda invests. When combined with the environmental fit (manifested as the need or value of such a core competence), this gives Honda a competitive advantage in the market for small engine offerings. As another example, Samsung is a South Korean company that has a core competence in the creation, design and manufacturing of video screen technologies. It uses this competence to deploy the technology in several different consumer product lines, like TVs, mobile phones and computer monitors. Note that some literature on the internet regarding Samsung states their core competences as "creative people, technology leadership, innovative culture, and customer value creation", but this is *really* just a collection of outcomes and assets. A true core competence describes what the organization can *actually* do with the combination of resources it develops and utilizes. The above is another example of how poorly worded strategic efforts can be; even of companies in the business of enacting them! The importance of utilizing core competences across businesses and products will be revisited in Chapters 11 and 12.

The VRIO Model

In Figure 3.1 we can see that competitive advantages (that is, being able to do better than your competitors and profit from that) can be explained by the unique combinations of assets, capabilities and competencies that an organization has at its disposal. However, that tells only half the story. It does not tell us, for instance, which assets, capabilities and competences are important for any particular situation. In fact, this initially led to criticisms of the RBV perspective as being tautological. A tautology is the repetition of an original idea using a different but comparable phrasing—the notion that something is something because it is something (i.e., a rose is a rose) … In essence, tautologies do not describe a true cause and effect relationship but merely say the same thing with different words. In the case of the RBV criticism, companies are successful because they have unique assets, capabilities and competences, and because they have these unique assets, capabilities and competences they are successful. But we need to know why they are *actually* successful and what leads to competitive advantage, which is usually measured in terms of above-normal profits for for-profit firms. The key is given by the clue in Figure 3.1—namely the notion of environment fit!

Indeed, assets, capabilities and competences are important because they allow us to fulfill some environment need (for example, to fulfill the market needs of consumers for a communication technology, etc., one would require a set of skills and assets in smartphone and internet technologies).

The key for your organization is that you must be the only ones (ideally) that can fulfill these needs in order to profit most from it. As such, the RBV model on organizational competitive advantage depends on these two concepts: (1) resource heterogeneity; and (2) resource immobility. That is, the resources are different across organizations and they may not transfer easily across organizations. The more that an asset, capability or competence is distinctive and the harder it is to transfer across organizations, the more strategic value it may create.

Jay Barney (1991) developed the VRIO framework, depicted in Figure 3.2, to explain how we might go about analyzing the potential of an asset, capability or competence to create a sustainable competitive advantage for an organization.

First, one identifies an asset, capability or competence to evaluate. The next question to ask is whether that asset, capability or competence is valuable. Here, as with much of strategic analysis, judgment is crucial and connection to the external environment "fit" is critical. In general, something is valuable if it allows the organization to exploit an opportunity or deflect a threat identified previously in our external analyses. An asset that either makes money or saves money would be valuable (note that there are also non-strategic assets that may not be valuable in this sense but are nevertheless required—for example, to meet regulatory requirements like doing your taxes. In these cases, such assets etc. would not be strategic and, though necessary, do not add to the bottom line profitably; in fact, in most cases they cost more money than they save …).

Given this definition of "valuable", any asset, capability or competence that does not give real value may lead to a competitive disadvantage, because the asset, capability or competence will still cost the organization but does not bring in any revenue to cover the costs. In general, one would want to eliminate any such non-essential asset, capability or competence (of course, the assets, capabilities and competences needed for compliance issues mentioned in the last paragraph will remain).

If the asset, capability or competence is considered valuable, the next question to ask is whether the asset, capability or competence is rare or unique to the organization. If it is, the organization will be able to build on it towards superior performance. If the asset, capability or competence is common then the best it can do for us is give us parity with our competitors, as they will be able to utilize a similar asset, capability or competence to do a similar thing to our organization.

Value and rarity relate to the notion of resource heterogeneity. In these cases, we may have a unique asset, capability or competence. However, if our

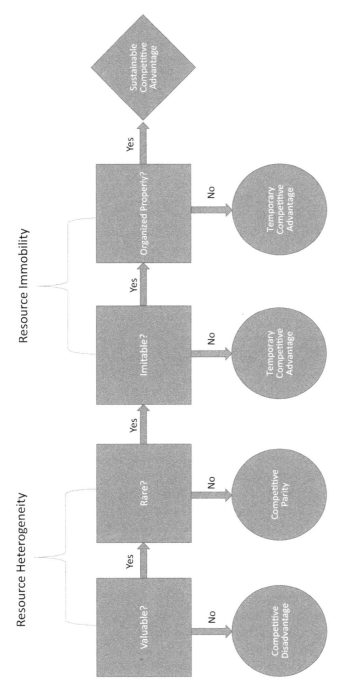

Figure 3.2 Ask yourself: Is the asset, capability or competence (valuable, rare, imitable and organized properly) for strategic advantage?

Source: Adapted from Barney (1991)

competitor is able to copy or substitute for the asset, capability or competence (with another asset, capability or competence) then any advantage will be quickly worn away. Thus, only when an asset, capability or competence is costly to imitate can that asset, capability or competence provide anything but a temporary competitive advantage. That is, it is only a matter of time before the asset, capability or competence that provided us with a competitive advantage is copied.

Finally, the last requirement for a sustained competitive advantage is that we must be able to organize the asset, capability or competence properly. If we own an asset, capability or competence that is valuable, unique and non-imitable then we may still not profit from it if we cannot truly use it properly … That would be akin to having a beautiful piano (an asset) but not being able to play it because of lack of other skills (competence in piano playing). Thus, the VRIO model suggests that overall success also depends on an interconnected web of other assets, capabilities and competences. An organizational example similar to the piano might be a company that has a sophisticated accounting software system, but no one employed who knows how to use it properly.

Internal Factor Evaluation Analysis

As we did in the last chapter but with a focus on the external environment, we can evaluate the importance of internal factors and how our strengths and weaknesses rate by creating an IFE analysis matrix table.

Again, one starts with a list all the factors identified as potentially important resources and capabilities for the industry we are in. Resources and capabilities that we currently have, and that are positive to our strategy, we can classify as strengths. Weaknesses are resources and capabilities that we either do not currently have or are not good at managing. Again, wording is important here. Strengths are things we are good at doing (i.e., capabilities) or things that we own that allow us to do things (i.e., resources). Weaknesses represent the lack of strengths (i.e., lack of "important" resources or capabilities).

Care must be taken in identifying true strengths and weaknesses. For example, often a root cause analysis is necessary to get at the true weakness rather than the result of underlying weaknesses. This is important, because the only way to fix a weakness (or take advantage of a strength) is to know it and enact upon it. For example, someone might state that our company's main weakness is poor product quality. From a layperson's perspective, this seems like a weakness, but what does this definition tell us about what we can do about this so-called weakness? Nothing. We must dig deeper to find the true weakness. A root cause analysis might suggest that it is poor material quality that is causing poor product quality, but we still don't know the true problem. Digging deeper, we find out the inbound inspection process is bad, ultimately because we lack qualified inspectors. We now have analyzed the problem back far enough to fix the true problem and our real weakness (i.e., we lack the valuable resource/asset of well-trained inspectors!).

The same can be said of products, which do not give competitive advantage themselves (even though most laypeople would think that is the case). Instead, we need to trace back via a root cause analysis to the true strengths, which can be things like having the best design team (asset) and great design practices (capability) that lead to creating successful products known for their design (e.g., Apple's iPhone). Products themselves can easily be imitated and often fail any VIRO test used on them. I discourage listing products and services (which are really outcomes) and actual outcomes like "profitability" and "market share" as strengths and weaknesses—unless you can argue that they can be utilized like a resource or capability (e.g., a brand) to build a competitive advantage.

Let's develop that internal factor evaluation matrix. In the IFE matrix, you assign a weight of importance to each strength or weakness in terms of strategic necessity—i.e., how important is the resource or capability to strategic success? The weight should represent the relative importance of the factor to the success of our main strategic goals. The total of the weights should equal 1.0.

Finally, rate each factor as to whether it is a major strength (4), minor strength (3), minor weakness (2) or major weakness (1). Note that strengths can be rated only with "3"s and "4"s, while weaknesses can be rated only with "1"s and "2"s. (This gives a spectrum of relative strength with regard to each resource or capability.) Finally, multiply the weights by the ratings and sum the resulting scores.

Table 3.3 depicts an example of an IFE matrix table with four to five items per resource type. Note that the final weighted score of 2.60 is slightly above the natural weighted average of 2.50. This is an indication that the current health of the organization towards enacting its strategy is strong. Now that you have taken a through and careful analysis of internal strengths and weaknesses, you have really earned your pay!

Table 3.3 Internal factor evaluation

	Description	Weight	Rating	Score
STRENGTHS				
1	Web-based technology skills	0.1	3	0.3
2	Experienced project manager	0.1	3	0.3
3	Extensive knowledge of the industry	0.05	4	0.2
4	Balanced top team in terms of experience	0.15	3	0.45
5	Proprietary technology	0.2	4	0.8
WEAKNESSES				
1	Interpersonal skills of managers	0.1	1	0.1
2	Foreign plant (lack of company-owned property)	0.1	2	0.2
3	Accounting skills (inexperienced)	0.05	2	0.1
4	Marketing skills (lacking needed knowledge)	0.15	1	0.15
		1		2.6

References

Barney, J. B. (1991). Firm resources and sustained competitive advantage. *Journal of Management*, 17(1), 99–120.

Hunt, S. D. 2000. *A general theory of competition*. Thousand Oaks, CA: Sage.

Hunt, S. D., & Morgan, R. M. (1995). The comparative advantage theory of competition. *Journal of Marketing*, 59(2), 1–15.

Wernerfelt, B. 1984. A resource-based view of the firm. *Strategic Management Journal*, 5(2), 171–180.

Part 2

Creating the Strategy

Strategic Formulation   4

Learning Objectives

By the end of this chapter, you will:

- Understand the concepts of strategic objectives—including what a vision and mission statement is;
- Comprehend the difference between an organization's vision statement and its mission statement;
- Understand how the main stakeholders of an organization can help determine an effective mission statement;
- Know what a TOWS analysis and TOWS matrix are.

Practice Objectives

By the end of this chapter, you will be able to:

- Create the elements of strategic objectives, including mission statement and SMART c3 measures;
- Analyze stakeholders and create a strategic stakeholder impact analysis (SSIA);
- Develop a TOWS analysis and TOWS matrix and create micro-strategies or tactics from them.

Techniques for Formulating Strategies and Micro-Strategies

Now that we have learned how to analyze the external and internal environments of any organization, we can begin the process of bringing the external and internal together, through integration, to create effective strategies.

Mission Statement (Re)creation and Strategic Objectives

Many textbooks on strategy begin by discussing the main objectives of an organization in the form of the mission statement—often assuming that this is the beginning of the strategic generation process. However, strategy, particularly for existing firms, can become a "chicken and egg" phenomenon, if not properly managed. The important point about objectives is that they are not the actual beginning of formulating strategy but, rather, should be the outcome of a preliminary strategic analysis emanating from the work generated in the processes of Chapters 2 and 3 as well as an analysis of stakeholders described in this chapter. In other words, you do not (usually) pick an objective out of the blue and base your strategy on that. Instead, effective strategy is generated by basing your objectives on concrete factual aspects related to your internal and external environments.

Let's start by defining strategic objectives. Recall the succinct definition of strategy introduced earlier as "the logic that links all the decisions made within an organization". As such, if logic is "the thinking behind decisions" then the objective is the final goal these decisions are meant to have us achieve.

As we learned in Chapter 1, there is a hierarchy to strategies and there is also a hierarchy to objectives. In general, most strategic objectives start with the vision of a single individual or team of entrepreneurs to offer something new to the world—be it a new product, a new service or a new design or idea. This often results in the vision statement, which is less a goal than an aspiration. As the name implies, vision statements are meant to communicate where the organization *aspires* to go in the future via its strategic implementation. It is mostly meant to *inspire* people within and outside the organization to move towards these ultimate goals. (One might say they are "inspirations towards aspirations".) However, quite often such visions are not necessarily achievable. In other contexts, we might call them "stretch goals"—things we may never attain but for which we will always strive. A classic example is Microsoft's original vision statement: "Putting a computer on every desk (in every house)". This is instructive for a number of reasons. First, Microsoft was, at the time, entirely a software company and did not sell computers. Two, the aspiration of a computer on every desk even today is unreachable. However, the "vision" helped to instill a sense of focus on making the computer (and, eventually, other consumer-driven electronics) more accessible. After all, computers without software to run them are useless. This image inspired people much more effectively then to state "We want to be the richest company in the world"—though it was to be that for some time …

As seen in Figure 4.1, the vision statement is the top of the hierarchy in strategic objectives. Like the layers of strategy, all the strategic objectives are related. The mission statement follows from the aspirations of the vision statement but is more concrete in its description of what the organization's main goals are to be. As shown in the next section, these goals need to relate to the main stakeholders of the organization. A mission statement is best written as a short paragraph of two or three sentences. However, despite being concise, or perhaps because of that, they may take an incredible amount of time to craft into an acceptable fashion. They involve extensive consultation with members within the organization about what the company should be doing and how they should be doing it. For our purposes, we will use an approach that is different from the "wordsmithing" that usually takes place. We will be more logical and methodical and focus on developing a mission that is *stakeholder-based*.

Figure 4.1 Hierarchy of objectives

A good mission statement is a document that guides how those in an organization should behave. It should be something that pays attention to the critical components and success factors in an organization and takes the interests of important factions within the organization into account. A mission statement should guide the behavior of individuals such that, if any individual makes a decision that is consistent with the mission statement, even if it is a poor decision, they will be supported for making that decision. As you can see, then, mission statements are critically tied to the creation and implementation of good strategy.

Aspects that may emanate from the enactment of a good mission statement are predicated on a number of more specific measures. First, we have critical success factors (CSFs), which are measures of important aspects of the organization's strategy that are *needed* for success. Careful definition of the CSFs is warranted. Note, CSFs are "things" needed for success, not the success (or outcome) itself. For example, the following three things—(1) develop accurate reports; (2) ensure reports are delivered in a timely fashion; and (3) create necessary reports to make business decisions—are all outcomes and not CSFs. Instead, one example of a potential CSF in this case might be "extremely powerful computers", so that efficient software analysis is available to generate those reports. Again, these are "things" (tangible, like computers, and intangible, like top management support) that, if one does not have as part of the organization, mean that success will be elusive. To be strategically focused only the top five CSFs for any planning unit is recommended.

The top key performance indicators (KPIs) are used to measure a strategy's performance directly related to the measures of corporate change. KPIs are those management indicators that are determined at the beginning of the strategic implementation and reflect directly on the key goals of the strategy. They are the basis for any tradeoff decisions during the course of the strategy's implementation. Finally, they should be measured in some way, at some time, on some scale.

KPIs and CSFs are distinctly different. The main difference is that CSFs are those things needed for successful strategy whereas KPIs are the measures of how well the strategy is performing. (The former is an input measure and the latter an output measure.) So, KPIs may spring from CSFs, but not the other way around. CSFs can be general and sometimes hard to quantitatively measure. One example of an amorphous CSF might be "top management support", which would be dichotomous—you either have it or not—and difficult to measure. You can also see in this example how a KPI would not apply. A strategy might need top management support to be successful but you would never measure top management support as a performance indicator of a strategy! So, one needs to be careful with the distinction between CSFs and KPIs. Although laypeople often use them interchangeably, they are different, and the difference *makes a difference* in how you might manage strategy.

Lower in the hierarchy and more numerous are the operating or tactical objectives, which measure the achievement of all the tactics that build up towards the overall strategic direction of the organization.

Effective tactical objectives use the SMART c3 format, an acronym made by taking the first letters of the following:

- **Specific**
- **Measurable**
- **Achievable**
- **Relevant**
- **Timed**

with a:

- caveat

and targeting measures at:

- three levels

A simple method for writing a SMART c3 objective is to first specify a verb, such as, for example:

- **Increase**

Then, specify the object of the verb:

- **sales**

by a measurable amount:

- **by 10 percent**

over a specific time period:

- **within six months**

while stating a major caveat or limitation

* **without reducing price**

Finally, give three levels of performance to capture the inevitability of variability:

* **10 percent good**
* **15 percent very good**
* **18 percent excellent**

This gives the SMART c3 objective: "Increase sales by 15 percent within six months without reducing price (but where 10 percent is okay and 18 percent is excellent)." Notice that all the SMART c3 requirements are included: The goal is specific and measurable; it is achievable, relevant to the company and timed; there is a caveat; and the three levels of performance are indicated (Johnson & Parente, 2013).

This is particularly important if performance will be judged by adherence to the objective. Many times we will be faced with performance measures that are unclear. For example, your boss might tell you that your goal is to increase sales. First, your idea of an acceptable increase may not be what their idea is. You may have increased sales by 15 percent and your boss decides that isn't enough. Understanding what is "good" in the beginning makes performance to the objective much easier. Another issue that is handled in the SMART c3 format is that of a time period. Once again, pre-specification is important, in that you will know that you have arrived at the "end" and thus the objective is completed. The caveat or limitation is perhaps the most different aspect of objectives. Frankly, anyone can increase sales by 100 percent if they don't have to be concerned about profitability. A caveat may be thought of as a limiting factor. It usually consists of a conflicting measure that keeps in check the measure that you are trying to manipulate in your SMART c3 objective. For example, you may want to increase sales but not at the expense of lowering prices so much that margins are eliminated and/or losses occur. Understanding caveats may be determined by asking questions such as the following: What will prevent us from achieving the specific objective? Is it lack of skilled personnel? Are business units competing for key resources that we also need? These may all become the caveats to achieving SMART objectives.

Stakeholders and the Strategic Stakeholder Impact Analysis

Stakeholders are any, and all, actors that are affected by and may affect the strategy of the organization. They are important to strategy because they may have a material effect on the success of our strategic goals. According to the philosophy of the Chicago economics school and Milton Friedman,[1] the only important stakeholder of a company is its shareholders. While these stakeholders are very important, history and experience have shown that other stakeholders can influence an organization's success, and managing their relationship with the organization is also paramount. Furthermore, not all organizations (for which strategy is just as important) are public companies.

As such, stakeholders can be broken into two general groups—internal and external—just like the strategic analysis factors discussed in Chapters 2 and 3. Anything that is outside the organization, over which management has little or no control, but may affect the organization, is external. Internal stakeholders are usually employees, but not always; for examples like partners and consultants, there may be an area of grayness. In general, anything over which we have some measure of control will typically be considered internal.

To conduct a stakeholder analysis, you must first identify the groups of stakeholders for an organization. Once groups are identified, it's important to categorize their key interests and concerns. This information will allow you to identify any claims that may be made by these groups. In addition, it is also important to ascertain which groups, from the perspective of the organization, are most important. These stakeholders' concerns will be of special interest. Finally, you should identify the resulting strategic challenges based on the information obtained.

The **interests** and **concerns** are what the stakeholder wants from the organization—at the most basic level. As an example, you need to put yourself in the shoes of the stakeholder and fill in the blank. The stakeholder is interested in _____ . For example: "The stockholders are interested in being paid dividends."

The **claim** is then the answer to a question of what the stakeholder will do if the planning unit does not respond to their interests or concerns. For example, if the firm does not provide dividends to the stockholders, they will move their investment to another firm. In all cases, the completion of the first four columns in the SSIA should be done similarly to Table 4.1, which depicts an SSIA on a case study of the introduction of a Bell Nortel network in a

Wors 1
↓ Case Scenario

Table 4.1 SSIA Example of Bell Nortel project strategy

Category	Stakeholder	Interest and concern	Resulting claim	Priority (1 = most important)	Strategic challenge
External	Mayor of Chapleau and City Council	Overall socio-economic improvement for everyone in the community	Deny access and resources and, essentially, kill project	1	Turn into project champion and solicit help when project roadblocks occur
External	Community organizations (e.g., Rotary Club, Canadian Legion)	Overall socio-economic improvement for everyone in the community	Use organization members to impede project progress	6	Present to each organization on the unique benefits from this new technology
External	School boards (three)	Enhanced education through broadband access	Seek other options or keep status quo	3	Help to envision possibilities, such as with case studies from other schools
External	Hospital system	Broadband internet that improves patient care and staff skill development	Seek alternative options	4	Convince hospital leadership of the probable benefits and introduce to other hospitals that have used broadband
External	Chapleau, Ontario, citizens	Affordable and reliable broadband internet access	Will use dial-up or cellular options	2	Deliver ideal broadband service and make it easy for each person to try at no cost
External	Aboriginal communities (First Nations)	Improved socio-economics for respective tribe/ nation	Will not adopt new broadband option	5	Demonstrate personal and business value from new broadband technology

External	Nortel CEO	10	Project success, improved brand sentiment and access to CRTC deferral funds	Terminate underperforming team members	Maintain frequent communications to understand project concerns from a CEO perspective
External	Bell Canada CEO	9	Project success, improved brand sentiment and access to CRTC deferral funds	Terminate underperforming team members	Maintain frequent communications to understand project concerns from a CEO perspective
External	Researchers	8	Observations that help to answer research questions	Will cancel research if project is delayed or weak content for a case study	Keep project on track and assist researchers in interviewing the right stakeholders
External	CRTC (Canadian Radio-Television and Telecommunications Commission)	7	Reliable telephone and other telecommunications services at affordable prices for all Canadians	Block CRTC funding to service providers; impose financial penalties	Prove that Nortel and Bell Canada are trying to provide quality telecommunications services at affordable prices to Chapleau and other towns in the future
Internal	Nortel project manager	11a	Project that is deemed a success and brings sustainable impact	Terminate or give poor reviews to team members hampering the project	Stay focused on the project success criteria and the defined strategies to achieve success

(continued)

Table 4.1 Cont.

Category	Stakeholder	Interest and concern	Resulting claim	Priority (1 = most important)	Strategic challenge
Internal	Nortel project operations	Efficient and effective project operations	Remove underperforming team members and give feedback to supervisor	12a	Deliver clear expectations as targets for desired network and application operations as well as frequent feedback
Internal	Network team	Clearly defined network and business requirements to design and operate the new network	Have a poor work ethic or quit their job	13a	Give proper constraints and objectives to deliver an excellent broadband solution that is adopted by the community
Internal	Applications team	Access to business issues and opportunities to solve with technology	Have a poor work ethic or quit their job	13b	Keep updated with feedback from Chapleau businesses and residents on opportunities to apply new broadband technology

rural Canadian town called Chapleau. See the case study by Edwards (2011) for more details.

The following is a simple statement of the relationship between stakeholder concerns and claims: The stakeholder is interested in <u>interests or concerns</u> (fill in the blank). The stakeholder will <u>make a claim</u> (fill in the blank), if their interests or concerns are not satisfied.

If you can complete this sentence by filling in specifics of the outlined words such that it makes sense for each of the stakeholders, you have probably done the exercise correctly.

You must also be sure to identify the stakeholder's interest and concerns at the most basic level. While there are politically correct answers, you should be sure to identify the interests appropriately. If you don't then you will not know how to develop a mission such that you will actually satisfy the stakeholder's needs. As an example, if a stockholder is interested in income, a firm should focus on producing excess cash to provide dividends. If stockholders are interested in long-term growth then the firm should invest excess cash from retained earnings to create additional value.

Another example concerns the employee as a stakeholder. While we might say that an employee is interested in having a great, ethical work environment, at the end of the day the employee may be most interested in long-term stable employment. Putting this in the format above:

> The employee is interested in *long-term stable employment*. The employee will *leave the company* if the firm does not provide long-term stable employment.

The next portion of the SSIA is a **priority** assessment. All the stakeholders are ranked according to the impact of their claims on the strategic success of the planning unit. Using the example of employee as a stakeholder, you will often need to subdivide the category for greater detail in order to be most effective. For example, when we think of a great research and development specialist leaving a firm, this might have a huge impact. We definitely do not want to ignore this stakeholder. However, when we think of a clerical employee leaving, one who is easily replaced, the impact is not as great and, essentially, could be ignored in terms of impact on the strategic direction of the company. Similarly, customers and employees are often thought of as critical resources, but you are encouraged to think critically as well as express interests at a basic level in order to make the correct priorities.

The final piece of the SSIA is to identify the **strategic challenges** in satisfying the interests and concerns and avoiding the claims of each stakeholder.

That is, how will the relationship with the stakeholder be "managed" to maintain goodwill and provide for their interests and concerns? Note that relationships with more important, high-priority stakeholders will be more challenging to manage. Once these are enumerated, it becomes easy to see where the overall challenges of the project actually are. This is where the strategy needs to focus.

Once the priorities are determined, the top three to five stakeholders should be used to develop the final mission statement. The philosophy is that inclusion of the top stakeholders in the mission statement will focus the development of new strategy correctly on the stakeholders with the most impact.

A mission statement emanating from our SSIA example of Table 4.1 might read something like: "The Bell Nortel project strives to develop enhanced broadband internet access for the overall socio-economic improvement of the government and people of Chapleau."

Note that this covers the concerns of many of the top stakeholders. One can, and often should, be more specific with things like what "socio-economic improvement" might mean. However, the mission statement's ultimate purpose is to communicate the general direction of the project and should be as concise as possible. One to three sentences that are carefully crafted to get the message right are ideal.

The TOWS Analysis and TOWS Matrix

As discussed so far, strategy is characterized by the matching of internal resources and skills and opportunities and threats created by external factors. Traditionally, this leads to a SWOT analysis that catalogues the *strengths, weaknesses, opportunities* and *threats* for an organization. The problem is that often the exercise leads to just that: a mere cataloguing of factors. What we want to do is take the IFE and EFE analyses of Chapters 2 and 3, which gave us the top ten factors of each category, and use these to actually create effective micro-strategies or tactics that will help us achieve our strategic goals. A TOWS analysis helps us do that.

TOWS analysis is a "structured brainstorming" technique that matches internal and external factors to illuminate potential strategies. Note that it is called TOWS rather than SWOT (a well-known iteration of the model) due to the fact that we start with the external factors first, because they give us the scenario that we must enact any strategies within. In other words, we are constrained by the external environment and less so by the internal. (Recall we have less control over the external factors.) The analysis leads to the creation of a TOWS matrix. _⟶ ℓ ⟋ ?_

The TOWS matrix is a two-by-two chart that depicts four types of strategies created by the combination of matching internal and external factors. These are SO, WO, ST and WT strategic alternatives:

- SO strategies use the project's internal strengths to take advantage of external opportunities. The strategic alternative is the response to the question: How can I use my internal strengths to take advantage of external opportunities?
- WO strategies take advantage of opportunities to overcome weaknesses. The strategic alternative is the response to the question: How can I take advantage of an external opportunity to overcome or improve the weaknesses?
- ST strategies use the project's strengths to avoid or reduce the impact of external threats. The strategic alternative is the response to the question: How can I use my internal strengths to avoid external threats?
- Finally, WT strategies are defensive tactics aimed at reducing internal weaknesses and avoiding environmental threats. The strategic alternative is the response to the question: What strategy can I develop that will help me to reduce an internal weakness and avoid the threat?

Table 4.2 illustrates a simple example of a TOWS for a telecommunication software and training company located in Singapore. "O"s and "T"s emanate from our EFE and "S"s and "W"s from our IFE analyses of Chapters 2 and 3. The resulting combination of factors results in various micro-strategies or tactics that the firm might use to enact its overall business strategy. For example, SO1 is a combination or "fit" between the opportunity (O1) and the strengths listed as S1 and S2.

Note that it is useful to list the factors that underlie the creation of the micro-strategy as depicted in Table 4.2. That is, (S1, S2, O1) at the end of the SO1 TOWS strategy makes it clear where the SO1 strategy came from.

At the end of the exercise a team can generate hundreds of TOWS strategies from the combination of top ten S, W, O and T factors. From that generative list the best options matching the overall strategy of the planning unit can be chosen for implementation. The way to determine the "best" options, of course, is to pick the ones that align most closely with the mission and strategic objectives determined earlier in the SSIA. Keep in mind that the TOWS strategies must be resourced (or paid for), so often you cannot implement them all. Usually the most prominent ones become clear but it is useful to

Table 4.2 Example of a TOWS matrix

	Strengths (S)	*Weaknesses (W)*
	S1: Geographical advantage—Singapore	W1: No Optimization Programming Language (OPL) product experience on the part of trainers
	S2: Academically qualified trainers	W2: Lack of lab equipment
	S3: Fluency in English and multiple Asian languages	W3: Inexperienced management team
Opportunities (O)	**SO strategies**	**WO strategies**
O1: Number of internet users in Asia is increasing	SO1: Take advantage of Singapore location to expand telecommunication training in Asia (S1, S2, O1)	WO1: Recruit highly talented trainers to overcome the trainers with no OPL product experience (W1, O3)
O2: Government support for knowledge-based industries in Singapore is increasing	SO2: Seek government assistance in setting up facilities (S1, O2)	WO2: Seek government assistance in funding lab equipment (W2, O2)
O3: Supply of qualified trainers in Asia is abundant		
Threats (T)	**ST strategies**	**WT strategies**
T1: Economic conditions in Asia are worsening	ST1: Use Singaporean trainers with foreign-language skills in other Asian countries to overcome the lack of confidence in local trainers (S3, T3)	WT1: Develop sales protocol for training programs that will identify the return on investment for OPL training in the poor economic situation (W1, T1)
T2: Customer expectations on service increasing		
T3: Lack of customer confidence in local expertise		

remain open-minded until the end. After all, recall that the TOWS analysis and resulting matrix are meant to constitute a brainstorming technique used to generate potential alternatives for strategic initiation.

Note

1 Milton Friedman writes, "There is one and only one social responsibility of business — to use its resources and engage in activities designed to increase its profits so long as it ... engages in open and free competition, without deception or fraud" (Friedman, 1962: 133).

References

Edwards, G. (2011). Bridging the digital divide: the case of a Bell, Nortel and Chapleau. *Case Research Journal, 31:3.*

Friedman, M. (1962). *Capitalism and freedom.* Chicago: University of Chicago Press.

Johnson, W. H. A., & Parente, D. H. (2013). *Project strategy and strategic portfolio analysis: A primer.* New York: Business Expert Press.

Developing a Global Strategy   5

Learning Objectives

By the end of this chapter, you will:

- Understand the stages of globalization for most organizations;
- Comprehend the strategic orientations for global operations and how industrial structures fit with them;
- Know financial and economic aspects for global strategy using the CAGE model;
- Understand the basic effects of exchange rates and transfer pricing strategic issues on global operations.

Practice Objectives

By the end of this chapter, you will be able to:

- Map out the stages of globalization for any organization;
- Determine the match between the strategic orientations for global operations of any organization and its industry;
- Create a CAGE model for comparing two or more countries or regions;
- Develop appropriate micro strategies for managing exchange rates and transfer pricing in any global operation.

Stages of Globalization

Although business and trade have been international for centuries—think the spice road linking China to the West, or the British East India Company, founded in 1600—the modern notion of the globalization of organizations is still fairly new. Early on, as international presence grew and was still dominated by US and British influences, much work on the globalization process focused on "eras" or "stages" in the process of globalizing. Figure 5.1 depicts the overall trends that led to the interconnected world of today. It was assumed most organizations started simply as extensions of their domestic operations. Sometimes referred to as "stages", which implies a hierarchy or level (with higher stages being higher levels of some trait), the term "era" also makes sense, because each era can be seen as the introduction of a new set of technologies and political/governance systems that allowed for an increase in globalization levels. In the first era, the creation of a "road" system linking the West with the East allowed for the introduction of pasta to Italy via China. The steam engine and industrial technologies led the way in the Industrial Revolution to provide the possibility for manufacturing on a scale for truly global production. Finally, the technological advancements in terms of the internet and communications ability allow for the instantaneous globalization of myriad companies selling digital products and services.

Indeed, as mentioned in the first chapter, the advent of the internet and instantaneous communication has allowed for the circumventing of the old continuous stages of global adoption. We now have the "Born Global" company, which is simultaneously global and domestic at its inception, as mentioned in the first paragraph of the book. Technological factors such as the internet and logistics (with decreased transportation costs and increased speed) have positively affected globalization. However, soft factors such as cultural integration and managerial skill development, which we discuss later in the book, constrain the ability to have instant globalization for any

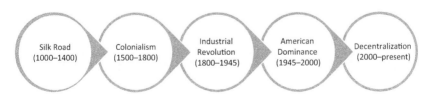

Figure 5.1 Five historical eras of globalization

Table 5.1 Stages of globalization for the typical company / organization

STAGES OF GLOBALIZATION STRATEGIES	MARKETS SERVED	IMPORTANCE OF CULTURE	TYPICAL PROGRESSION OVER TIME
Domestic	Mostly home market	Not important	Begin exporting
International	Exports increase	Important	Initial move
Multinational	Int'l Sales > 30%	Very important	After international
Global	Int'l Sales > 80%	Critically important	After international
Transnational	Int'l Sales > 90%	Critically important	Last move

organization. Thus, even Born Global companies may have to experience the managerial process as "stages of development", as shown in Table 5.1.

In other words, most companies start focused on the domestic market—where thinking about "different" cultures and market preferences that may be unusual to the entrepreneur is not necessary. However, as the percentage of sales from foreign sources increase and the stages advance from international through to transnational as depicted in Table 5.1, the importance of understanding novel cultures and attitudes (not to mention other novel and foreign institutional factors) becomes critically important.

Strategic Orientations and Industrial Structures

Research on the basic strategies that organizations tend to utilize has identified two major pressures that organizations must deal with when managing their global network. These basic strategies resulted in the integration–responsiveness framework of global strategic orientations (Prahalad & Doz, 1987; Roth, Schweiger & Morrison, 1991). The two major pressures are: (1) pressure to reduce costs/increase integration of the global network (i.e., integration); and (2) pressure to respond flexibly to local market tastes (i.e., responsiveness).

The cost pressure often involves minimizing cost by centralizing functions, but the aspect of integration (linking and streamlining the functions within the organization) is also important, and hence the term "integration" is often used to describe these pressures. That is, we ask the question: Does it make most sense to integrate and consolidate as much of the organization's functions as possible (versus allowing for more flexibility)? This is usually associated with cost, because flexibility is expensive. Integration, when done right, can help reduce costs. But, ultimately, it is integration that is key: All companies will have pressures to decrease costs but not all need (or can) integrate functions.

The responsiveness pressure stems from differences in consumer tastes and other external aspects of the regional and local environment. Thus, in some countries a certain brand or offering may be preferred. In some countries the technological system may require flexibility (e.g., in electrical outlets and characteristics of the electricity grid). In these cases, the organization may need to manage the appropriate responsiveness in terms of flexibility.

As can be seen in the descriptions of these two pressures, namely integration versus responsiveness, they are often at cross-purposes. One reduces costs and the other increases it; or, the one increases flexibility and the other decreases flexibility. Placing the two pressures on a two-by-two grid gives the integration–responsiveness framework of global strategic orientations, depicted in Figure 5.2. Clearly, there are four basic strategic orientations that emanate from each quadrant's 'position' vis-à-vis the combination of the two pressures for an organization. Each strategic orientation can be linked with the global strategy of any particular firm; an example is listed in Figure 5.2. Listed below the firm is an example of some industries that typically utilize such a strategy. Indeed, the industrial structures of many industries naturally follow from their specific integration and responsiveness pressures.

Thus, the "Global (standard)" strategy[1] exists when the pressure for integration is high and the pressure for responsiveness is low. Such a strategy

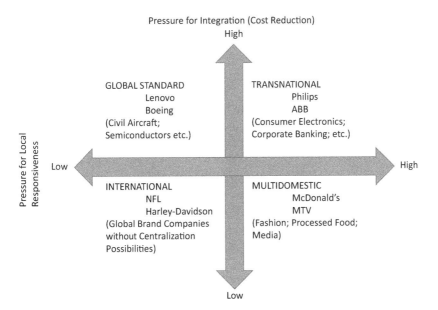

Figure 5.2 Integration-responsiveness framework of global strategic orientations

attempts to centralize (integrate) many of the organization's functions. Ideally, for example, the organization's offering or product can be produced centrally in one or two locations, taking advantage of global economies of scale and sold as a "generic" offering worldwide. This is the ideal "global product"—produced cheaply and sold worldwide without much differentiation. In reality, no product or service allows for complete global integration. However, offerings that are commodities or highly specialized and expensive to produce, and for which large economies of scale are necessary, tend towards the "Global standard" strategy. Civil aircraft manufacturing companies like Boeing and Airbus fit into this latter position.

The "International" strategy exists when the pressure for integration is low and the pressure for responsiveness is also low. In such cases there is no need to change the offering, nor is there much pressure to integrate functions to decrease costs. Of course, note that this does not mean that management might not want to decrease costs, but in cases when pressure for integration is low the ability to centralize production may be limited and therefore no cost pressures (due to integration!) exist. Despite being the first strategy many newcomers choose for globalizing, few companies or organizations can inhabit this space for long. Examples like the National Football League (NFL) and Harley-Davidson, both from the United States, are brand-oriented organizations that do not find the need to change their offerings when they enter foreign markets; indeed, changing the offerings may dilute the very value proposition such companies offer. In many cases, neither is there the ability to lower costs due to integration. The NFL, for example, cannot centralize its players, who are distributed across individual teams in the league. The premium price of Harley motorbikes decreases the necessity for production integration, and in some cases production in a country is required or desired for market entry. An example would be the Japanese automobile manufacturers that opened plants in the United States in order to seal their entrenchment in the American marketplace.

The "Multidomestic" strategy exists when the pressure for integration is low but the pressure for responsiveness is high. The lack of integration pressure is similar to the "International" strategy. That is, pressure for integration is low and the ability to centralize production may be limited, such that few cost pressures to integrate functions exist. This may be due to a limitation of physical factors, such as in the case of the food industry, where perishability of many products is an issue, and so one requires warehouses fairly close to the final marketplace. However, organizations facing "Multidomestic" strategies do feel pressure to change their offerings depending on the foreign market they are in. Offerings that may relate to cultural preferences and unique local tastes are prime suspects for "Multidomestic" strategies. As such, companies in food, fashion and media industries often enact such strategies.

The "Transnational" strategy exists when the pressure for integration is high and the pressure for responsiveness is also high. This creates a heightened tension, because organizations in such situations will want to both centralize functions and create economies of scale as well as differentiate the offerings of local regions. Industries like consumer electronics fall into this quadrant, where many companies will centralize production, as best they can, but also change offerings for local taste or requirements. Hewlett–Packard's printers provide a simple example of such a strategy, whereby Hewlett–Packard centralized the production of its printers and created generic plugs into the printers while changing the prongs and transformers of its electric input cords. This is why the cord for many printers and computers is not permanently attached to the unit but, rather, plugs into both the electronic device and the electrical outlet. It allows for centralized production of the unit but also flexibility in the variable electricity requirements for different regions of the world. As such, "Transnational" strategists try to centralize or integrate the things that they can but also add flexibility to the things that they must, due to local market pressures. Needless to say, this strategy (while attempting to have the "best of both worlds") can be extremely difficult to implement.

These integration–responsiveness strategies are not predetermined prophecies. Despite the natural tendencies of some industries towards specific strategies, the ultimate strategy enacted by the organization depends on the decisions made by its top management. In general, the strategy of any particular organization may be unique and create its own strategic advantage. As mentioned, the tendency is always towards cost reduction, so when integration is actually possible most organizations try to implement strategies that integrate functions. The choice of whether to respond to local demands can be strategically based and up to the organization itself. For example, when KFC first entered Japan its regional manager quickly offered other food items besides chicken, such as fish, which suited the traditional Japanese diet. Initially corporate KFC in the United States was intent on a "Global standard" strategy; after all, at the time the company was not yet called the more inclusive "KFC" but "Kentucky Fried Chicken", and, as its name implied, was all about that type of meat. The regional manager from the United States was replaced after a while by his Japanese protégé. Only later, after more multicultural studies had shown the importance of local responsiveness and KFC had diversified its menu items, did the company enthusiastically embrace the "Multidomestic" strategy. Today KFC and other fast food giants, like McDonald's, usually offer a diversified menu based on the company's global

Table 5.2 Pros and cons of each integration–responsiveness framework strategy

Strategy	PROS	CONS
Global standard	Low costs due to focused production	No local responsiveness
	Economies of scale due to standardization	Little product differentiation
		Some exchange rate exposure
		Some potential for IP violations / expropriation
International	Low costs (exporting; franchising; trademarks)	Limited to no local responsiveness
	No need for differentiation	Potential for IP violations / expropriation
	Economies of scale	
	Leverages core competences	Sensitive to exchange rate fluctuations
Multidomestic	Low sensitivity to exchange rate fluctuations	High costs due to functional duplications
	Increased ability to differentiate	Few to no economies of scale
	Increased propensity of local changes to offerings	High potential for IP violations / expropriation
		Little to no learning / synergies across regions
Transnational	Economies of scale combined with focus on location advantages	Costly to implement
		Some exchange rate exposure
		High potential for IP violations / expropriation
		High failure rate

Note: IP = intellectual property.

staples as well as unique regional menu items. In India, McDonald's does not sell beef, because Indians hold the cow in sacred esteem and are offended by the thought of eating beef.

Table 5.2 describes some of the pros and cons of each of the integration–responsiveness framework strategies.

Financial and Economic Aspects of the Globalized Firm Related to Strategy

Building upon the PESTEL model of Chapter 2, there are a few specific regional financial and economic factors that will affect the development of an organization's global strategy. We'll look now at using the CAGE model to compare across country and regional elements, as well as bottom of the pyramid markets and economic distance. Finally, we touch upon the phenomenon of transfer pricing, which is an inherent part of a globally networked organization, and the ever-present exchange rate effects.

CAGE Model

The acronym of the CAGE model stands for cultural, administrative/political, geographic and economic factors. The main difference between this model and the PESTEL framework from Chapter 2 is that it focuses on apparent differences or "distance" between two specific countries, usually the home country of the organization being analyzed and a country that is a candidate for entry. While the PESTEL framework can help determine trends that underlie the opportunities and threats of a foreign market, the CAGE model illustrates the fitness for aligning the business of the home country with that in the foreign country. That is, countries that are closer in "distance" tend to find it easier to do business with each other. PESTEL shows us the potential opportunities and threats of the market while CAGE tells us whether entering the market might be considered reasonable or not.

The CAGE model was first delineated by Pankaj Ghemawat (2001). "C" stands for "culture". In general, cultures are closer (i.e., in cultural distance) when the two countries share common languages, political systems and religions. A lack of similar ethnic or social networks and trust or mutual respect between countries will increase "cultural distance" and make it harder to trade with one another. Industries and products that are most affected by cultural distance often relate to linguistic content in media and entertainment, for example. Religious identity and country-specific associations such as regional brands (think Champagne and Gouda or Cheddar cheese) may also be most affected. We will expand more on aspects of national and regional culture later, in Chapter 6.

"A" stands for "administrative" (also similar to the "political"). Administrative/political factors affect the ease of business, and the more similar the institutional structures of the two countries are, the easier it is to do business. A shared trading bloc, shared currencies and ratified trade agreements help decrease distance. A good example is the European Union (EU) trading bloc, where the use of shared currency and trade policies eases trade between EU countries. Colonial ties and similar financial and legal institutions also decrease administrative distance. For example, many of Brazilian institutions will share commonalities with those in Portugal, because the former is an ex-colony of the latter. Similarly, Kenya has many institutions akin to the British system. Industries and products that are most affected by administrative distance are critical resources like utilities, as well as defense-related, national security areas like telecommunications and aerospace.

"G" stands for "geographic". Geographic distance is the most intuitively obvious (in terms of being a "distance" concept), although the model considers not just physical "distance by land" but also other differences in terms of climate and time zones, etc. A lack of a common border, waterway access, adequate transportation or communication links, physical remoteness and different climates and time zones will all increase geographic distance. Countries with similar climates (despite physically being a world apart) will be closer in geographic distance and generally find it easier to do business with each other. One reason is because climate can determine the shared need for similar products (e.g., clothing or food). Hot climates differ from cold climates; the former tend towards using spicier foods (due to the historical lack of refrigeration) and the latter require warm clothes to survive the cold. In terms of physical distance, industries and products that are most affected by geographic distance are those with a low value-to-weight ratio (like cement) or those that are fragile or perishable (e.g., fresh foods). Ghemawat (2001) also sees geographic distance as relevant when communications between countries are vital (such as in financial services).

Finally, "E" stands for "economic". Economic distance is the difference between socio-economic status for two specific countries. Different consumer incomes, differences in the cost and quality of natural, financial and human resources, different information or knowledge and varying consumer tastes will all increase economic distance. Obviously, products for which demand varies by income (such as luxury goods) and industries in which labor and other cost differences matter (e.g., in textiles and agricultural markets) will be most affected by economic distance. Economic distance may also explain how some countries can seemingly "work together" more effectively and efficiently than others. For example, many African countries have found it easier to work with Chinese firms than American firms within their borders because of the closer "economic distance", with China still being considered an emergent economy even in the face of its massive size and recent economic growth.

Economic Distance Issues: The Bottom of the Pyramid (BoP) as a Source for Global Opportunities

As can be seen with the last factor of the CAGE model and with the description of Chinese expansion into Africa, economic distance can have a profound effect on global business. While most trade takes place between countries of similar economic development, particularly in terms of finished goods as opposed to commodities and raw material inputs, there is now more and more recognition that the lower-status economic population may provide substantial business opportunities. C. K. Prahalad has popularized the term "bottom of the pyramid" (Prahalad & Hart, 2002; Prahalad, 2004) to describe the poorest socio-economic group, around 2.7 billion people who live on less than $2.50 a day, as a potential consumer group. This is because, while this group is poor, it is also the largest "consumer" grouping of people in the world. The key to business opportunities for the BoP groups is that the offerings must match the needs and ability to pay for this consumer group. This has led to the concept of lean innovation, in which innovations are designed for or emanate out of the experiences of the BoP environment. Everett Rogers (2003) discovered five attributes of an innovation that affected its adoption: relative advantage, complexity, compatibility, observability and trialability. Studies suggest that the first two—relative advantage and complexity—may be most important to the BoP marketplace. Technologies that meet perceived needs without frivolous extras and are less complex than other technologies seem to do well in BoP markets. Cellphone adoption has actually been quicker in economies characterized by BoP because of the lack of a need for a more complex communications network of land lines. For example, cell towers are easier to install and result in cheaper networks than older wired networks. (Recall the example of M-PESA in Kenya.) While the CAGE model applies to the ease of doing business across countries in general, the BoP idea also shows us that economic opportunities may still exist across the economic spectrum. However, as pointed out in Chapter 1 when discussing the entry of Western companies into China, businesses need to carefully understand the unique needs and positions of lower-income BoP economies.

Exchange Rates and Transfer Pricing Strategic Issues

When doing business globally it is inevitable that different financial and monetary systems need to interact. Whether or not a company deals exclusively with one currency for its own accounting purposes, it will still need to consider exchange rates when dealing with local currencies. Exchange rates, essentially, determine how much one currency can buy in another currency. For example, how many US dollars are needed to buy a euro? While we don't cover the calculation of exchange rates in this book, it is important to point out that exchange rates (and their fluctuations) can have a profound effect on the measure of strategic success for any global strategy an organization enacts. Recall the factor of luck (or chance) in strategy from Chapter 1. Luck, unfortunately, can go both ways: both bad and good. If the exchange rates between two economic trading blocs fluctuate greatly, what was once a good profitable business venture might become a financial disaster. For example, if our Indian company was buying material from a Canadian company for C\$10/lb. and the exchange rate increased the Canadian dollar by 10 percent relative to the Indian rupee, instantly our material costs would rise by 10 percent, to C\$11/lb—and all of this despite no change in management practices or strategies. In other words, this change is all about luck—and, in this particular case, bad luck.

Thus, the long-term implications of economic and currency fluctuations need to be considered when organizing a global network. Obviously, the CAGE model can help here (where economies that are closer in administrative, political and economic characteristics have fewer potential shock), as well as choosing markets that are less prone to economic shocks in general—garnered from a thorough PESTEL analysis.

When a company has various foreign subsidiaries the issues of transfer pricing becomes important, particularly when the company trades across borders with itself. There are micro strategies in and of themselves for effective transfer pricing. Done right, the process can save substantial money, with overall tax obligations lowered, but there are rules and regulations that govern when and where specific policies can be utilized. Specialized accounting firms like Ecovis Global offer help in setting up such transfer pricing policies. Essentially, transfer prices must be like what would occur in an arm's-length transaction; that is, in a sale between entities that are not related but independent entities and with equal power. Here, consulting the accountants is of paramount importance.

Note

1 The original framework called this strategy the "global" strategy, but this obviously causes confusion when the framework itself is called the global strategy orientation of the firm. As such, newer renditions use the term "global standard" or "global standardization".

References

Ghemawat, P. (2001). Distance still matters: The hard reality of global expansion. *Harvard Business Review, 79*(8), 137–147.

Prahalad, C. K. (2004). *The fortune at the bottom of the pyramid*. Philadelphia, PA: Wharton School Publishing.

Prahalad, C. K., & Doz, Y. L. (1987). *The multinational mission: Balancing local demands and global vision*. New York: Simon & Schuster.

Prahalad, C. K., and Hart, S. L. (2002). The fortune at the bottom of the pyramid. *Strategy+Business, 26*, 54–67.

Rogers, E. M. (2003). *Diffusion of innovations* (5th ed.). New York: Simon & Schuster.

Roth, K., Schweiger, D. M., & Morrison, A. J. (1991). Global strategy implementation at the business unit level: Operational capabilities and administrative mechanisms. *Journal of International Business Studies, 22*(3), 369–402.

Part 3

Implementation Issues for the Global Strategy

The Important Aspect of Culture   **6**

Learning Objectives

By the end of this chapter, you will:

- Understand the nature of culture;
- Comprehend the differences in national, sub-national and corporate cultures;
- Know the models of culture developed in management—namely Hofstede's model and the GLOBE study;
- Understand that care needs to be taken in avoiding too generalized stereotypes and prejudicial assumptions when using culture models;
- Understand the effects of culture on implementing a global strategy.

Practice Objectives

By the end of this chapter, you will be able to:

- Define the basis of culture;
- Determine the cultural positions of a country and region using the Hofstede and GLOBE models;
- Create a comparison analysis of two or more countries based on the Hofstede and GLOBE models;
- Appropriately utilize notions of culture in the upcoming chapters in terms of differences in communications and business practices worldwide.

What Is Culture?

Culture is one of those elusive terms that we all seem to understand but can't quite grasp; we see it everywhere but often find it hard to define. Researchers define culture as the underlying shared values and traditions of a specified group of people. As such, culture can apply to many different levels of "groupings" of people. It could be national, regional, organizational or even within one family unit. The key terms when defining culture are "shared" and "values". The elusive nature of culture is engendered in the onion model of culture seen in Figure 6.1.

Essentially, what we all "see" of a culture is often the outward appearances that reflect that culture. These are the artifacts and rituals of any particular culture—that is, the outer layer of the culture. But, as we dig deeper, we get closer to the meaning of those artifacts and rituals, and, essentially, the shared values of that culture, based on an implicit assumption or philosophy. The notion of being implicit is important, because often people act the way they do for reasons of which they are not explicitly aware. To this extent, culture drives behavior in semi-autonomous ways (i.e., people often automatically behave a certain way because of their innate cultural beliefs). For example, many Japanese people bow because, traditionally in the Japanese culture, bowing has been a form of showing respect. In the West, the default gesture for respect upon meeting someone is a handshake (in the United States with one hand, in some countries two).[1] In both cases, our culture helps determine

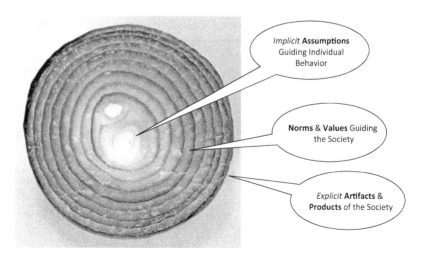

Figure 6.1 Onion model of culture

what actions we might apply in any social situation. Some argue that, while we can see the outer layer of the onion (i.e., the artifacts and rituals of a culture) quite easily, the basic assumptions are often not even knowable to those in a specific society or culture. Thus, it may be dangerous to assume, especially for an outsider, that one knows the true underlying basic assumptions of any culture. To some extent, we are all biased as to what we can see rather than what is implied.

One reason for studying national culture is to develop cultural awareness and, hopefully, create cultural empathy. At the very least, as one studies different cultures one will get an appreciation for different viewpoints on how to do things and what is important to others in the world. In many cases, though not always, people are open to outsiders' indiscretions when it comes to cultural niceties like the handshake, which can differ in firmness and degree across the world. The key to cultural empathy is to understand that differences exist and to accommodate those difference when possible. This is why the expression "Travel broadens the mind" is so correct. Traveling the world gives one a personal view into other cultures. It can also help lessen the potentially damaging aspects of creating and utilizing stereotypes that are "too general".

Stereotypes are widely held views on the artifacts and values of any particular culture. While there is usually some underlying truth to a stereotype, it is often the case that stereotypes are overly simplified versions of the truth, and when used in a racially biased or prejudicial manner often verge on absurdity and ignorance. Because stereotypes are generalizations it is false to assume that all individuals in a culture exhibit the same traits. For example, while the kilt is a traditional garb of the Scottish and a well-recognized artifact, not all people from Scotland wear kilts. The stereotype is something we need to keep in mind when thinking about culture such that we need to guard against too broad generalizations while keeping the benefits of being able to categorize group behavior.

Effects of Culture on Global Strategy

Interestingly, if we go back to the general definition of strategy as the "logic linking all decisions of an organization", we can see the connection with culture. Metaphorically, the shared values are the vision or mission of a group of people (e.g., a tribe), and the actions linked to those shared values are a kind of strategy. Before we get too ahead of ourselves with this metaphor, the key is that culture will have an overwhelming influence on our strategies, and this is why it is so important to study it when implementing global strategy. On a simple level, *if a cultural norm does not allow for an action that is essential for a strategy, that strategy will fail in that culture.* Basically, we will need to take cultural or value-oriented factors into account in implementing our global strategies, which we explore in the rest of this book.

National, Sub-national and Corporate Cultures

As mentioned, culture as "shared value" can be categorized into a number of differently defined groups or organizations of people. For global strategy, we are generally interested in three levels: the national, sub-national (or regional) and corporate. The national is one of those levels where we often feel that we know what it is but may be too comfortable in our own knowledge. The case of the Scottish kilt is exemplary again. While we often think of Scotland and the kilt simultaneously, that form of dress is actually traditionally associated with the Scottish Highlands. Thus, sub-national or regional cultures are important and may dominate (or not) at the national level, depending on politics and other power struggles within the national border. An often cited issue with African country politics is that most African countries were created by European powers that did not consider regional tribal lands at the time. This has created tensions and warfare, seen in, for example, the splitting of Sudan into southern and northern entities.

In business, sub-national cultures might be more important than national-level indications. For example, in the United States the two coastal regions to the West and East are often labeled the "Left Coasts", primarily by political rivals who wish to point out the urban, more liberal nature of each coastal region. However, the culture of East Coast New York is quite different from West Coast Los Angeles, as anyone who has traveled to each can attest. Thus, even within a country, sub-national regions might need to be managed differently.

Finally, because we are interested in cultural interactions due to implementing our organizational strategy, the internal corporate culture of our organization also needs to be considered in any implementation analysis. Organizations are groups of people, and as such will exhibit their own "shared values and traditions". Indeed, the organizational culture (synonymous with the term "corporate culture" here) will be directly related to the organizational strategy, as reflected in statements of the last section. For example, if our firm's strategy is to be the "low-cost producer" in our industry, for us to be successful we must have a culture that is cost-focused with everything that we do and think about being focused on lowering costs. The founder of Walmart, Sam Walton, famously stayed in cheaper motels when traveling for business, to personally "model" the value of thriftiness in Walmart's culture. For a low-cost producer strategy, moving production into a region that has values that are not focused on such an "efficiencies perspective" may result in failure. In such a case, cultures that "value" time off and other social benefits that add costs may need to be managed more tightly than cultures that are more cost- and efficiency-aware. As such, both our organizational culture and organizational strategy need to align with the cultures of the regions in which we would like to operate for optimal performance.

Models of National Culture

We will focus on two of the most pervasive models of national culture used today. Both are widely utilized to examine differences across nations and both have some flaws. One thing to keep in mind when using such measures is that culture does, in fact, change. There is some evidence that the bowing behavior in Japan mentioned earlier may be waning in the younger Japanese generation, which has been exposed so much to the Western culture of handshakes and waving in similar situations. Of course, as I finish this edition of the book the Covid-19 pandemic is just happening, and changing the use of the handshake to waving and elbow bumps. This is an indication of how significant events can change actions and cultures.

Hofstede's Model

Geert Hofstede is a researcher from the Netherlands who is well known for studying national cultures, as he produced one of the first cross-cultural comparisons of different nations starting in the 1970s. Essentially, Hofstede was working for IBM, one of the most internationalized companies at the time, and was able to survey employees from around the world to determine differences in cultural attitudes and values (Hofstede, 1991). He defined culture as "the collective mental programming of the human mind which distinguishes one group of people from another".[2]

While there have been criticisms of the methodology, with some arguing that the IBM corporate culture dominated differences in national culture and with arguments of the stereotyping of national identities, the model is seen as good for comparing across nations and determining cultural distance (as seen in the last chapter). Initially, Hofstede discovered five dimensions, with one being characterized as Confucian dynamism or related to Asia cultures,[3] but more work and surveying since then have extended the dimensions to six and replaced Confucian dynamism with a time perspective. We'll run through the six dimensions here.

Power distance (PD) is "the extent to which the less powerful members of organizations and institutions (like the family) accept and expect that power is distributed unequally" (Hofstede, 2011: 9). Power is perceived from the followers, and it is their acceptance that creates this "value". A higher degree of PD indicates that power and hierarchy are accepted, without doubt, and a lower degree of PD that the culture is more egalitarian in nature. As Hofstede points out: "All societies are unequal, but some are more unequal than others" (ibid.: 9).

Individualism versus collectivism (IDV) is the "degree to which people in a society are integrated into groups" (Hofstede, 2011: 11). Individualistic societies are populated with members who have loose ties to each other and tend to emphasize "I" versus "we" in their thinking patterns. Collectivist societies are populated with members who have a strong tendency towards "in-group" connections (often based on extended family) "that continue protecting them in exchange for unquestioning loyalty, and oppose other ingroups" (ibid.: 11).

Uncertainty avoidance (UA) is defined as "a society's tolerance for ambiguity" and, as pointed out by Hofstede, "is not the same as risk avoidance" (ibid.: 10). Cultures high in UA tend towards more formal codes of behavior to avoid the uncertainty that may be seen in one's actions. Low-UA cultures may be more open to new and different ideas. Hofstede (2011: 11) states that people from these cultures

> are more tolerant of opinions different from what they are used to; they try to have fewer rules, and on the philosophical and religious level they are empiricist, relativist and allow different currents to flow side by side. People within these cultures are more phlegmatic and contemplative, and not expected by their environment to express emotions.

Masculinity versus femininity (MAS) is a dimension that separates cultures based on how they emphasize what it means to be successful within that culture. Masculinity is defined as "a preference in society for achievement, heroism, assertiveness and material rewards for success". Femininity, on the other hand, demonstrates "a preference for cooperation, modesty, caring for the weak and quality of life". While there is more to the MAS dimension than gender issues, the role of women does seem to differ between the two extremes of the masculinity and femininity poles. According to Hofstede (2011: 12), "Women in feminine countries have the same modest, caring values as the men [but] in the masculine countries they are somewhat assertive and competitive, but not as much as the men."

Long-term orientation versus short-term orientation (LTO) measures the emphasis a culture places on time in its decision-making and actions. Again, Hofstede comments that

> values found [for LTO] were perseverance, thrift, ordering relationships by status, and having a sense of shame [while] values at the opposite, short term pole were reciprocating social obligations, respect for tradition, protecting one's "face", and personal steadiness and stability.
>
> (ibid.: 13)

One way to understand this is to reflect that people in short-term-orientated societies believe that "most important events in life occurred in the past or take place [in the present]" while in long-term orientated societies "most important events in life will occur in the future" (ibid.: 15). For business purposes, this has meant that faster economic growth has been associated with long-term orientation. That is, unless one believes that an investment will make money in the future, why invest when one can spend that money now?

The newer dimension of indulgence versus restraint (IND) has been described as a "measure of happiness" within a culture. A high-indulgence culture "allows relatively free gratification of basic and natural human desires related to enjoying life and having fun" while a high-restraint culture "controls gratification of needs and regulates it by means of strict social norms" (ibid.: 15). A ramification of indulgent culture is that people believe they control their own destinies and therefore have free will in their actions. Restrained cultures believe more in fate and predetermined destinies, exhibited in the expressions "God willing" or "God's will". In such a culture, what happens to someone is often seen not of his or her doing but, rather, the will of God. Restrained societies are less "happy" than indulgent ones and, interestingly (given the emphasis on lack of free will), tend to have a higher number of police officers per capita!

Hofstede's model can be used to compare countries with one another on the scaled indices just described. In theory, the closer the distance between two countries on each and every index, the easier it should be to conduct business. Thus, Hofstede's model can be used as one measure for use in

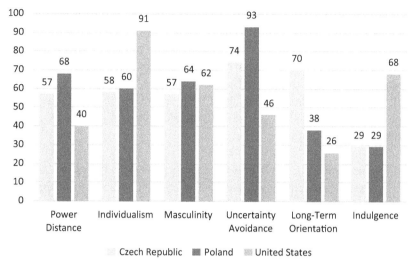

Czech Republic ■ Poland United States

Figure 6.2 Hofstede's dimensions for the Czech Republic and Poland
Source: Data sourced at www.hofstede-insights.com

the "Culture" element of the CAGE model from Chapter 5. For example, Figure 6.2 depicts the index scores from Hofstede for two former Soviet bloc countries, the Czech Republic and Poland, and the United States. Essentially, the bloc countries are very similar cultures except perhaps on the UA and LTO, which may help explain the slightly better economic development of the Czech Republic in recent years.

However, when we include the dimensions' scores for the United States, we can clearly see that the similarities are much closer between them than with the United States, which, interestingly, does quite well economically despite a short-term orientation.[4] Differences in UA and LTO would require significant thought about how to manage operations in each country and are probably an indication that different incentive structures and leadership styles might be required. More on these issues later …

Figure 6.3 depicts a two-by-two graph that can show distance between countries based on two of Hofstede model dimensions—in this case, UA and PD. Here, we could easily categorize countries into four categories or quadrants: (1) high PD and low UA; (2) low PD and low UA; (3) low PD and high UA; and (4) high PD and high UA. Countries within the same category could be considered "close distance" countries with similar managerial practices. For example, Brazil and Portugal are both in quadrant 4. Not surprisingly, after studying the CAGE model, we can recognize many shared characteristics; e.g., both countries' inhabitants speak Portuguese, because Brazil was a Portugal colony.

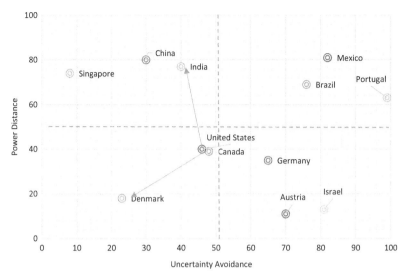

Figure 6.3 Measuring cultural distance with Hofstede's dimensions

Source: Data sourced at www.hofstede-insights.com

The United States and Canada are very close on these indices and both are within the low UA/low PD area (quadrant 2). (Again, both were British colonies at one time.) One can also use such graphs to map out the vector distance between countries. That is, even though they are within the same category, Canada is much closer to the United States in cultural distance on these measures than is Denmark (see the arrow). Let's say the United States is at position (40,46) while Canada is at (39,48) and Denmark is at (18,23) for position (PD, UA). The absolute difference from the US position is measured for Canada as (–1,+2) and for Denmark as (–21,–25). Using Pythagorean theorem, we can calculate the vector distance (length of the arrow) as 2.8 and 34.7, respectively.[5] Comparing to India, the absolute difference is (37,–6) and the vector distance is 37.5; despite being close in UA to the United States, the power distance difference is substantial, which makes for a potential major cultural impediment to doing business between the United States and India compared to the United States and Denmark.

The clustering of cultures, inherent in the data of Figure 6.3, can also be seen in Figure 6.4, which depicts the tendency towards regional clusters of shared cultural values. The countries included in the cartological graph are the ones analyzed in Figure 6.3. This is a potentially useful tool in analyzing differences and similarities in cultural values. Note that clusters, again, appear to share language, legal and colonial ties, etc. The clustering is based on data from Gupta, Hanges and Dorfman (2002), who categorized countries into

Figure 6.4 Cultural clusters

ten clusters: Anglo, Latin America, Latin Europe, Eastern Europe, Germanic Europe, Nordic Europe, Sub-Saharan Africa, Arab, Southern Asia and Confucian Asia.

GLOBE (Global Leadership and Organizational Behavior Effectiveness) Model

The GLOBE model is another national culture survey meant to focus more specifically on issues of leadership and organizational effectiveness rather than merely national cultural values.[6]

The study, initiated by Robert House in the 1990s, resulted in nine GLOBE cultural orientations, some of which are very similar to Hofstede's. They are defined as follows:

- **Performance orientation:** The degree to which a collective encourages and rewards (and should encourage and reward) group members for performance improvement and excellence.
- **Assertiveness:** The degree to which individuals are (and should be) assertive, confrontational, and aggressive in their relationship with others.
- **Future orientation:** The extent to which individuals engage (and should engage) in future-oriented behaviors such as planning, investing in the future, and delaying gratification.

- **Humane orientation:** The degree to which a collective encourages and rewards (and should encourage and reward) individuals for being fair, altruistic, generous, caring, and kind to others.
- **Institutional collectivism:** The degree to which organizational and societal institutional practices encourage and reward (and should encourage and reward) collective distribution of resources and collective action.
- **In-group collectivism:** The degree to which individuals express (and should express) pride, loyalty, and cohesiveness in their organizations or families.
- **Gender egalitarianism:** The degree to which a collective minimizes (and should minimize) gender inequality.
- **Power distance:** The extent to which the community accepts and endorses authority, power differences, and status privileges.
- **Uncertainty avoidance:** The extent to which a society, organization, or group relies (and should rely) on social norms, rules, and procedures to alleviate unpredictability of future events. The greater the desire to avoid uncertainty, the more people seek orderliness, consistency, structure, formal procedures, and laws to cover situations in their daily lives.

(http://globeproject.com/study_2004_2007)

The GLOBE study also identifies six characteristics of leadership. It defines leadership as "the ability of an individual to influence, motivate, and enable others to contribute toward the effectiveness and success of the organizations of which they are members" (House, Hanges, Javidan, Dorfman & Gupta, 2004). From the study they discovered what they term "culturally endorsed implicit leadership (CLT)" as styles associated with different cultures. The six are as follows.

(1) **Charismatic/value-based leadership:** Reflects the ability to inspire, motivate, and expect high performance outcomes from others based on firmly held core values. It includes the following six primary leadership dimensions: (a) visionary, (b) inspirational, (c) self-sacrifice, (d) integrity, (e) decisive, and (f) performance oriented.
(2) **Team-oriented leadership:** Emphasizes effective team building and implementation of a common purpose or goal among team members. It includes the following five primary leadership dimensions: (a) collaborative team orientation, (b) team integrator, (c) diplomatic, (d) malevolent (reverse scored), and (e) administratively competent.

(3) **Participative leadership:** Reflects the degree to which managers involve others in making and implementing decisions. It includes two primary leadership dimensions labeled (a) nonparticipative and (b) autocratic (both reverse-scored).

(4) **Humane-oriented leadership:** Reflects supportive and considerate leadership and includes compassion and generosity. This leadership dimension includes two primary leadership dimensions labeled (a) modesty and (b) humane orientation.

(5) **Autonomous leadership:** Refers to independent and individualistic leadership attributes. It is measured by a single primary leadership dimension labeled autonomous leadership, consisting of individualistic, independence, autonomous, and unique attributes.

(6) **Self-protective leadership:** Focuses on ensuring the safety and security of the individual and group through status enhancement and face saving. It includes five primary leadership dimensions labeled (a) self-centered, (b) status conscious, (c) conflict inducer, (d) face saver, and (e) procedural.

(http://globeproject.com/study_2004_2007)

As can be seen in the description, the GLOBE study is useful for determining how to best provide leadership for a particular culture, which we return to in later chapters.

Final Note on Cultural Models

Other models of national culture do exist, such as Fons Trompenaars' model. These are all somewhat similar but sometimes slightly different from the Hofstede and GLOBE models. This chapter is not meant to be an all-inclusive and comprehensive examination of such models. For expediting purposes, I focus only on the two most often used by practitioners and academics. You should explore the internet for models that may be useful for your purposes. For example, we will examine Trompenaars' in more detail in Chapter 8, because he developed a national culture model that is explicitly useful in examining organizational structures across nations.

Furthermore, as expressed in Figure 6.5, there are other environmental factors that affect managerial practice (see Deresky, 2014). We have already explored the macro environmental factors of national economic and political variables, for example, as well as the socio-cultural variable of language and

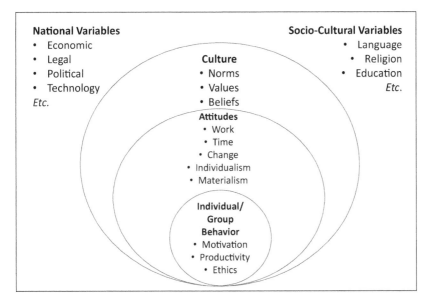

National Variables
- Economic
- Legal
- Political
- Technology

Etc.

Socio-Cultural Variables
- Language
- Religion
- Education

Etc.

Culture
- Norms
- Values
- Beliefs

Attitudes
- Work
- Time
- Change
- Individualism
- Materialism

Individual/ Group Behavior
- Motivation
- Productivity
- Ethics

Figure 6.5 Environmental factors that affect managerial practice

Source: Adapted from Deresky (2014)

religion as seen in the CAGE model. However, as depicted, cultural variables are at the center of these factors and color the perspective of leaders, followers, managers and employees. This is seen in the all-encompassing connection of culture with the attitudes and behaviors that we find within an organization (as aspects therein show in Figure 6.5). As such, a systems perspective must be taken into account; that is, all factors must be considered simultaneously in a large model of management practices, and this will differ for any specific situation.

As mentioned before about stereotypes and relying too much on generalized data for a population, one needs to be careful when applying national culture models. First, things change over time (although culture itself can be very rigid, it can be changed slowly—usually, if at all, generationally and by a process that is called "punctuated equilibrium". This is a hypothesis that evolutionary development is marked by isolated episodes of rapid "change" between long periods of little or no change.). Second, not all situations can be reduced to the generalization of survey data. In implementing real strategies, visiting the country and meeting the people who will be your customers or employees is vital to understanding whether your globalized strategy will work with the national and sub-national cultural environment.

Notes

1 See the link here for some examples of different ways of handshaking in the world: http://mentalfloss.com/article/54063/what-proper-handshake-etiquette-around-world (last accessed April 3, 2020); the effects of the Covid-19 currently wreaking havoc in the world will no doubt discourage handshaking in general.
2 See www.hofstede-insights.com/product/compare-countries for more insight and tools for Hofstede on analyzing national culture (last accessed April 3, 2020).
3 Interestingly, China (the home of Confucius) was not included in the original list of countries, because IBM, at the time, was not invested in China and so Hofstede had no data on that country.
4 This reflects on the rather low propensity towards savings for Americans. Many investments tend to be short-term in nature.
5 Using Pythagoras—i.e., $a2 + b2 = c2$—one can calculate the length of the vector. The distance of the line between the United States and Canada is $\sqrt{((-1)^2 + (2)^2)} = \sqrt{(1 + 4)} = \sqrt{5} = 2.2$ and Denmark is $\sqrt{((-21)^2 + (-25)^2)} = \sqrt{(441 + 625)} = \sqrt{1066} = 32.6$.
6 See http://globeproject.com for more information on the GLOBE project (last accessed April 3, 2020).

References

Deresky, H. (2014). *International management: Managing across borders and cultures: Text and cases* (7th ed.). New York: Prentice Hall.

Gupta, V., Hanges, P. J., & Dorfman, P. W. (2002). Cultural clusters: Methodology and findings. *Journal of World Business*, *37*(1), 11–15.

Hofstede, G. (1991). *Cultures and organizations: Software of the mind*. London: McGraw-Hill.

Hofstede, G. (2011). Dimensionalizing cultures: The Hofstede model in context. *Online Readings in Psychology and Culture*, *2*(1). https://doi.org/10.9707/2307-0919.1014.

House, R. J., Hanges, P. J., Javidan, M., Dorfman, P. W., & Gupta, V. (eds.) (2004). *Culture, leadership, and organizations: The GLOBE study of 62 societies*. Thousand Oaks, CA: Sage.

Cross-Cultural Communication

7

Learning Objectives

By the end of this chapter, you will:

- Understand the nature of communication;
- Comprehend the unique importance of communication to implementing global strategy;
- Know the different types of verbal and non-verbal communications;
- Understand the differences in communication qualities around the world;
- Understand the effects of communication on implementing a global strategy.

Practice Objectives

By the end of this chapter, you will be able to:

- Define the basis of communication;
- Determine the verbal and non-verbal communication traits of cultures across the world;
- Create a comparison analysis of two or more countries based on verbal and non-verbal communication traits;
- Appropriately utilize notions of verbal and non-verbal communication traits in the upcoming chapters in terms of business practices worldwide such as negotiation techniques, managing employees and contracting with business client and partners.

What Is Communication?

We all want to get our messages across to others, from the time we are babies trying to tell our parents that we'd like to have our next meal, please … But getting the message across, even in our own cultures, is always difficult work. We define communication as a process of creating and sharing meaning by transmitting messages via media such as words, behavior or material artifacts. This can be accomplished through verbal communication, like the use of a language (linguistics), or non-verbal, like use of signs (semiotics). It is important to point out that non-verbal can include use of semiosis—signs—many of which are not based on language per se. The use of color, for example, can be used to transmit meaning without using words and can be considered symbolic in nature and culturally dependent.

There are always at least three elements of any communication: (1) the sender (you); (2) the receiver (your target audience); and (3) the message itself (which can take many forms like an email, verbalization or perhaps a simple gesture—among others). However, this means that the intended message of the sender is predicated on the understanding of that message by the receiver. Unfortunately, there are many places in which the meaning of the original message can be distorted. Anything that undermines the communication of an intended message is referred to as noise.[1] Noise exists because people filter messages consistent with their own expectations and perceptions of reality, as well as their values and norms of behavior. Culture colors these expectations and perceptions. As such, the more dissimilar the cultures of those involved, the more likely it is that misinterpretation will occur.

The Importance of Communication to Global Strategy

The last sentence of the previous section points out the importance of understanding communication when managing global strategy. Again, recall the CAGE model and this issue of language. A shared language is always useful when integrating across cultures. However, it is important to emphasize that not all communication is verbal. When determining cultural distance, aspects of communication (discussed next) are important to include in the analysis. Sometimes, within a culture, what is **said** is *not* always what is **meant**. Sometimes what is said can be construed as the opposite of what was meant. In Japan, for example, it is well known that people often reply "Yes" as a sign of respect and of confirming that they heard the message and **not** of having agreed with the message.

As such, it is important first to realize that different cultures may have different communication styles. Second, it is necessary to study the cultures and communication styles of the foreign lands in which we are interested in investing our time and money.

Types of Communication

Communication can be broken into two main types: (1) verbal communication; and (2) non-verbal communication.

Verbal Communication

Language is the major element of verbal communication. Understanding another language and effectively communicating is an important aspect of managing across borders; however, even within the same language group, subtleties and regional differences can exist. French in Upper Canada is different from French in Paris. In fact, *interestingly*, Parisian French is newer than the French used in the Old Quarters of Montreal and Quebec. Being open to understanding these differences is a start towards developing the cultural empathy discussed in Chapter 6. In general, it will help if the sender of a communication (you) initially explores the situation for any subtleties by requesting feedback in communications. Some cultures are more explicit in their communication styles, and we'll explore this in a later section.

Trust can be important to developing effective verbal communication. When trust exists, cultural misunderstandings may be considered less rude and more acceptable. However, trust takes time to develop between parties, and, like many factors, the propensity towards trusting others varies across cultures as well. High-"trusting" cultures, such as Nordic countries, the United States and the United Kingdom, may be more prone to accepting cultural *faux pas* than lower-"trusting" cultures, such as Romania and Turkey. A *faux pas* is an embarrassing act or remark in a social situation; usually predicated on a misunderstanding or lack of knowledge in a situation. A famous example of a *faux pas*, saved by a gracious reaction, was when a guest of Britain's Queen Victoria mistook the lemon water used to clean one's hands at the end of the meal for a drink (the initial *faux pas*). To save face, the queen promptly picked up the bowl and drank a sip with a nod to her guest. Perhaps the story is apocryphal, but it certainly shows a great sense of cultural empathy and general humanity.

Non-Verbal Communication

Much communication is perceived at the level of the subconscious. The wink in an eye (for two lovers) or the color of a shirt (think brown shirts, for the Nazis) can instantly create an image in the receiver's mind. Clearly, non-verbal communication can constitute many of the messages that we receive daily. Non-verbal communication is the transfer of meaning through mechanisms such as body language and gestures, semiotics or the use of non-verbal signs and the use of physical space.

Figure 7.1 is a photograph taken by the author on a trip to China of what appears to be an electrical transformer box of some kind. It serves an interesting study in communication. One can see that there is both Chinese and English script written on it, so we have an example of written communication. While the English translation is somewhat humorous, the message is clear: Don't touch! The use of the "caution" sign, with thunderbolt, helps to reinforce the message and is an example of the use of semiotics. The light on the left is red and the one on the right is green. These red and green lights are likely color-based signs of the activity of the electrical box. Finally, the placement of the plant on top provides a logical paradox in communication.

Figure 7.1 Communicating danger on many levels!

Clearly, we should not "touch the power", but one can't help thinking what might happen to the poor person who decides to water this plant while the electricity is flowing in the box below! This is, clearly, multi-leveled communication at work.

There are several groupings or types of non-verbal communications:

> **Chromatics**, as seen in the example of Figure 7.1, is the use of color to communicate messages. In the West, the color red is often used to symbolize danger, and so Westerners may perceive the red light in Figure 7.1 as meaning that the power is on and touching the box would be dangerous. For driving, stop lights and stop signs are red for a reason. However, green lights often mean that power is on, so the use of color in this example is potentially problematic. (Again, green means "go" throughout the world when driving.) Yellow and black in nature, the colors of the bumblebee, can also mean danger, such that the caution sign of Figure 7.1 (which is in yellow and black!) is also instructive.

Color meaning can—like all things, it seems—vary by culture. For example, traditionally red in China does not mean danger but joy, and is the color of celebration. Historically, brides wore red, though the increasing use of white in Chinese weddings is a sign of the mixing of global cultures. It is also indicative that local context also matters rather than just national context. White in China traditionally symbolized death (it is the color used in funerals), so the mixed messages of the Chinese wedding are apparent![2]

Kinesics is the study of communication using body movements, including gestures and facial expressions. In cross-cultural communications, gestures are an important aspect of kinesics. As with colors, the same gesture in different parts of the world can have different connotations associated with it. The peace sign gesture ("V" sign) in the United States is an insult in Britain when the "V" of the index and middle fingers is displayed with the palm facing towards the person giving the sign. The traditional okay sign with the thumb and index finger forming an "O" is used throughout the world as a positive symbol of satisfaction but it recently has been usurped by white supremacists as a symbol of that less than okay movement. Similarly, the original symbol coped by the Nazis as the swastika is a centuries-old Hindu symbol representing lasting eternity and peace … One can see the original, unchanged symbol in many places in Asia, which some Western visitors find shocking given their own cultural background.

The meaning of facial expressions also can differ around the world. While smiles generally mean happiness in most cultures, a smile can also communicate other messages depending on context. Furthermore, not everyone is used to smiling in social situations. The Chinese and Russian cultures are well known for traditionally lacking the use of smiling in communications. In fact, Russians were taught how to smile at guests as part of their training for the Olympics and the FIFA World Cup event in 2018!

Eye contact and postures are also kinetical and differ across the world. Some cultures find direct eye contact, particularly in high-distance cultures, untenable (see Hofstede's model from Chapter 6), while others, such as in the United States, see lack of eye contact as a sign of a lack of trustworthiness or a lack of confidence. You can see in this example how models of cultural differences relate to, and may help explain, some communication preferences. Postures such as leaning over someone will have a different interpretation in a high- versus low-power-distance cultures and depend on who is doing the leaning.

Proxemics is the study of the use of physical space, and the distance between the sender and receiver, in communications. In general, there are four levels of distance: (1) intimate (used for confidential whispering of a message); (2) personal (used for communicating with close friends and family; (3) social (used when communicating with acquaintances, as in most business transactions); and (4) public (used when making a presentation to a group of people). The distances used will vary often between cultures. For example, some professors like to make group talks more intimate by traveling the room and getting closer to the audience, which is accepted in some informal-based cultures. Others, in more formal cultures, want the professor to stand behind a lectern and be more "distant" from the audience.

Finally, **chronemics** is the study and use of time perception in communication. This also differs across cultures. For some cultures, being on time is imperative. Being a minute late or too early is seen as rude and can convey a message that the sender does not care. Other cultures have a huge fudge factor in their sense of time—such as the famous "ish-time", as in "Let's start our meeting around '4-ish'", which could mean anything from 3:30 until 4:30! Some cultures cherish the notion of being "fashionably late", though much can depend on the power structure of the relationships involved. (Remember, the boss might be late, but you cannot use his or her example as a basis for your own tardiness!)

Two general perceptions of time in cultures have been elucidated: (1) the monochronic time schedule, whereby things are done in a linear manner and the emphasis is getting things done on time; and (2) the polychronic time schedule, whereby several things are done at the same time and people place a higher value on personal involvement than on getting things done on time.

Non-verbal communication is vast. Some believe that more is *not said* then is *said* in our daily communications, for all cultures. Other examples of types of non-verbal communication include haptics (touch) and vocalics (paralanguage, or how people speak, such as in speed of talking and volume); these can all communicate messages, and may differ worldwide. The key to global strategy and non-verbal communication is to understand once again that differences in perception and use of such non-verbal communication exist across the globe. So, non-verbal communication is another important aspect that the global strategist must consider in implementing global strategy.

Cultural Communication Styles

All messages involve context and it is an important element of any communicated message. However, the importance of context differs with culture.

High- versus Low-Context Cultures

Context is the notion of the background that all communications takes place within. Noam Chomsky's famous studies of syntax and sentence structure show us that the meaning of a sentence may depend heavily on the context or background in which the sentence is made. For example, the statement "This is a man eating shark"[3] will have a different meaning if it is spoken within a fish restaurant versus beside an aquarium's shark tank.

Figure 7.2 illustrates the relationship between the degree of context for communications and the explicitness of communications for various cultures/countries (Hall & Hall, 1990). Note that the relationship is linear and produces a diagonal line. High-context cultures utilize heavily context-based and implicit communications. For example, in Japan, who the sender is and who the receiver is are as important as the message being sent. There are some things that the junior Japanese sender can never say, even if he or she wanted. Communications are implicit and indirect, with voice intonation, the timing of the message and facial expressions conveying important information about the message. Especially in Japan, the use of silence is multi-faceted, with the lack of words conveying important messages (Rösch & Segler, 1987: 60). Communications of any mode in such high-context cultures are tied up in social connections and interrelationships with traditions and history.

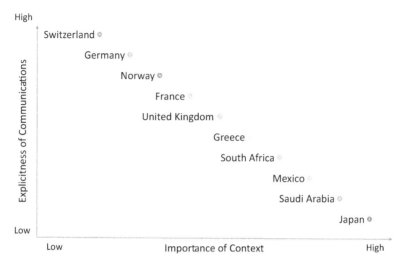

Figure 7.2 Countries and mapping to context and explicitness of communication
Sources: Deresky (2014); Hall & Hall (1990); Rosch (1987)

Contrarily, low-context cultures, such as Germanic-based ones, have explicit communication styles. Words expressed are made as direct and focused on the objectives of the message—as much as is possible. In Germany, a father might say "You are my son, and I want you to do something for 'this' and 'that' reason", whereas, in Japan, a father might allude to a metaphor of patriotic duties to one's elders to get his message across to his son, including use of silence.

The notation of low and high context is a general indication of the importance of context in a society for communicating. High-context societies can be difficult to communicate in by people who are used to explicit communications. The use of orders and instructions in managing people from different types of contextually based cultures will need special attention. We'll see later, in Chapters 9 and 10, how this might affect management at the operating level of a global strategy.

Four categories of verbal styles can further be elucidated (see Table 7.1) (Francesco & Gold, 1998).

(1) **Direct** (A) versus **indirect** (B) styles, with the former being explicit and the latter implicit regarding the message spoken.
(2) Degrees of communication quantity are broken into three categories: elaborating (A), exacting (B) and succinct (C). **Elaborating** style uses excessive speech and is used often in high-context cultures, with a moderate degree of uncertainty avoidance. This contrasts with the **succinct** style,

Table 7.1 Characteristics of various verbal styles

Category	Verbal style	Type	Style description	Typical cultural background	Importance of context
1	**Direct**	A	Explicit messages	Individualistic	Low
1	**Indirect**	B	Implicit messages	Collectivistic	High
2	**Elaborate**	A	High quantity of talk	Medium Uncertainty Avoidance	High
2	**Exacting**	B	Moderate amount of talk	Low Uncertainty Avoidance	Low
2	**Succinct**	C	Low amount of talk	High Uncertainty Avoidance	High
3	**Contextual**	A	Focus on roles	High Power Distance	High
3	**Personal**	B	Focus on personal relationships	Low Power Distance	Low
4	**Affective**	A	Focus on receiver and emotional content	Collectivistic	High
4	**Instrumental**	B	Focus on sender and sender goals	Individualistic	Low

Source: Adapted from Francesco & Gold (1998)

also popular in high-context cultures, with considerable uncertainty avoidance, wherein people say few words and allow understatements, pauses and silence to convey meaning. We often think of high-context cultures by the latter description because we feel context speaks volumes in high-context cultures. However, it is important to state that high context does not mean low verbal quantities or that a high number of words are used in messages. Saudi culture is an example of high-context-elaboration style, in which context is important and, while the words spoken may not be direct, they are often voluminous. Japanese is classically a high-context-succinct style culture. Finally, the **exacting** style focuses on precision and the use of only the appropriate number of words to convey a message.

(3) Verbal styles can concentrate on the roles of the communicating actors, called **contextual** (A), or the personal relationships between communicating actors, called **personal** (B).

(4) Finally, verbal styles can focus on the receiver and the message's emotional content, called **affective** (A), or focus on the sender and the sender goals, called **instrumental** (B).

Table 7.2 Verbal styles across ten countries

Country	Verbal style (category from Table 7.1)			
	1	2	3	4
Australia	A	B	B	B
Canada	A	B	B	B
Denmark	A	B	B	B
Egypt	B	A	A	A
Japan	B	C	A	A
Korea	B	C	A	A
Saudi Arabia	B	A	A	A
Sweden	A	B	B	B
United Kingdom	A	B	B	B
United States	A	B	B	B

Source: Adapted from Francesco & Gold (1998)

Table 7.2 lists the verbal styles of ten different countries. Can you find the countries that match each other on all four? Theoretically, the closer the match across all four styles, the easier communication is across those cultures. There are only three basic types: (1) ABBB (European/American); (2) BAAA (Middle Eastern/Muslim); and (3) BCAA (Asian).

History, Communication and Getting the Message Wrong

The importance of communication (and understanding the history and context behind images and words, etc.) is very clear in the marketing of products and services across country borders. For example, the clothing fashion design store Zara once sold a "Sheriff's" shirt in the United Kingdom, Israel, Germany, France, Albania and Sweden, among others, that, unfortunately, reminded some people of the uniform worn by Holocaust victims. A spokesperson stated, "The garment was inspired by the classic Western films, but we now recognize that the design could be seen as insensitive and apologize sincerely for any offence caused to our customers." The obvious similarity of a sheriff's star badge to the Star of David and the connection with the Jewish Holocaust of the Second World War should have triggered warnings in the marketing department. While Holocaust victims wore vertical stripes and the Star of David, one commenter suggested that getting rid of the stripes (and perhaps having "Sherriff" written on the badge emblem) may have alleviated the problem.

Even when only words are used, mistakes happen. Pepsi's "Come alive with Pepsi" advertising campaign—so successful in the United States—was translated into Chinese as "Pepsi brings your ancestors back from the grave"!

Bottom line (note the directness): One needs to take care communicating in any and all situations.

Notes

1 Even within one's own social group, noise can distort the message as anyone know if they've played the 'telephone game' in which many people pass a message along through a chain—one to another to another, etc.—passing it along with a whisper into the next person's ear. The original message usually is changed along the way.
2 See the website https://allegravita.com/2011/01/17/color for interesting color meanings in China (last accessed April 3, 2020).
3 Note that, in written communication, adding the "-" (a hyphen) to "This is a man-eating shark" can help make the distinction clearer for this example, but note that the spoken sentence will still depend on context to elucidate its meaning.

References

Francesco, A. M., & Gold, B. A. (1998). *International organizational behavior: Text, readings, cases, and skills*. Upper Saddle River, NJ: Pearson Education.

Hall, E. T., & Hall, M. R. (1990). *Understanding cultural differences: Germans, French and Americans*. Yarmouth, ME: Intercultural Press.

Rösch, M., & Segler, K. G. (1987). Communication with Japanese. *Management International Review, 27*(4), 56–67.

Managing Structure   8

Learning Objectives

By the end of this chapter, you will:

- Know the various organizational structures used for global strategies and operations;
- Comprehend the link between strategy and structure for each of the structures and strategies used in global operations;
- Know the different types of organizational strategies associated with different parts of the world, identified by Fons Trompenaars;
- Understand the use of control mechanisms in managing organizational structures and how this may differ in different parts of the world.

Practice Objectives

By the end of this chapter, you will be able to:

- Define organizational structure;
- Determine which organizational structure is most appropriate given the position of a company in terms of its global strategic orientation;
- Determine which organizational culture is most appropriate or likely given the location of a company in terms of Trompenaars' model;
- Create a potential organizational structure recommendation for any global strategy chosen to be implemented.

What Is Organizational Structure in the Global Context?

Organizational structure is a systematic way of depicting the rules, roles and responsibilities of internal members of an organization. Often depicted using an organizational chart that displays information flows within the organization, the organizational structure also shows reporting characteristics—that is, who reports to whom. In short, it shows us the formal flow of information for any specific organization.

In a globalized organization the information flows can become complicated, and quite often the official organization chart, which is the formal depiction of internal information and reporting flows, is not what is actually enacted. Indeed, Henry Mintzberg and Ludo Van der Heyden came up with the concept of the "organigraph" to depict what actually is happening within any organization that the formal org. chart does not show, including interactions with important stakeholders outside the organization (Mintzberg & Van der Heyden, 1999).

First and foremost, a firm's org. structure must "fit" with its strategy and be conducive with its implementation. We'll see this later in this chapter when comparing organizational structures to the global strategic orientations from Chapter 5. The choice of structure will be contingency-based by taking into consideration factors such as the firm's size, the appropriate technologies utilized, the organizational environment, geographic dispersion and the differences in time, language, cultural attitudes and business practices within its global network. Given the complexities, it is often more difficult to develop and implement/enact the appropriate organizational structure than it is to develop the strategy itself.

Structural Arrangements in Global Strategies

The initial structure utilized by many organizations new to globalization is the simple divisional structure. Here, one might have a simple export arrangement, which is common among manufacturing firms, especially those with technologically advanced products. The creation of on-site manufacturing operations is often in response to local government requirements for domestic production when sales increase. It is also useful for reducing transportation costs to the foreign market. Local subsidiaries are also common for finance-related businesses and other businesses that require a domestic service or legal presence. Figure 8.1 depicts a simple international division with a

Figure 8.1 Simple divisional structure

Figure 8.2 International division structure

dedicated unit to all managing overseas operations. As the name implies, this is possible only when foreign operations are relatively simple and duplicative over the markets where the organization is active.

The international division structure, illustrated in Figure 8.2, handles all international operations out of a division created for this purpose. It ensures that the international focus receives top management attention, because the international division manager reports directly to the CEO and therefore provides a unified approach to international operations. It is often adopted by firms still in developmental stages of international business operations. However, it separates domestic from international managers, and thus it can be difficult to act strategically as a unit and allocate resources effectively on a global basis.

The global product division, seen in Figure 8.3, is a structural arrangement in which domestic divisions are given worldwide responsibility for product groups. Global product divisions operate as profit centers, and this helps them better manage the particulars of their product, technologies used to offer it and the diversity of the customer base such that it can best cater to local needs. Marketing, production and finance are coordinated on a product-by-product global basis.

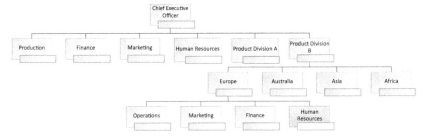

Figure 8.3 Global product division structure

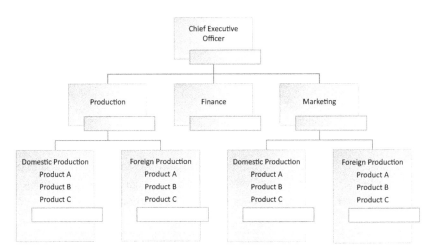

Figure 8.4 Global functional division structure

This structure can result in the duplication of facilities and staff personnel within divisions. Detrimentally to the corporation as a whole, the division manager may pursue currently attractive geographic prospects and neglect others with long-term potential. They may also spend too much time tapping local rather than international markets.

The global functional division structure, seen in Figure 8.4, organizes worldwide operations primarily on the basis of function, and then on product lines as a secondary feature. The structure is not often utilized but is used by companies in areas such as oil and mining exploration. It is favored only by firms needing tight, centralized coordination and control of integrated production processes and firms involved in transporting products and raw materials between geographic areas. The structure emphasizes functional expertise and centralized control with a relatively lean managerial staff.

Figure 8.5 Global area division structure

Figure 8.6 Multinational matrix structure

However, downsides include the fact that coordination of manufacturing and marketing can be difficult. In addition, managing multiple product lines can be very challenging, because of the separation of production and marketing into different departments.

The global area division structure, shown in Figure 8.5, is utilized where global operations are organized on a geographic basis. That is, international operations are put on the same level as domestic, with global division mangers responsible for all business operations in designated geographic area. It is often utilized by companies with mature businesses and narrow product lines. It allows the firm to reduce costs per unit and to price competitively by manufacturing in a region.

However, it is difficult to reconcile a product emphasis with the geographic orientation. For example, new R&D efforts are often ignored, because divisions are selling in mature markets and do not emphasize the product approach.

The multinational matrix structure, seen in Figure 8.6, is a combination of the global product, area and functional structures. It allows the organization to create a precise type of design that best meets its specific needs. For example, in Figure 8.6 we have local area managers that have both a product outlook (on industrial goods) and an area or regional focus in terms of the market. However, as a matrix design's complexity increases, coordinating personnel and getting everyone to work towards common goals often becomes difficult. A major issue is the "two bosses" problem, when there are too many reporting authorities, and difficulties can arise in agreement on where to focus (and whom to please).

Finally, the transnational structure arrangement combines elements of function, product and geographic design, while relying on network arrangements to link worldwide subsidiaries. At the core of the transnational network structure idea are nodes, which are units charged with coordinating product, functional and geographic information. Different product line units and geographic area units have different structures depending on what is best for their particular operation. Thus, the transnational structure attempts to maximize: (1) the capabilities and resources of a multinational corporation (MNC); (2) the economies of scale of a global corporation; (3) the local responsiveness of a domestic company; and (4) the ability to transfer technology efficiently, which is typical of the international structure. This, obviously, becomes difficult to do well.

The transnational structure, depicted in Figure 8.7, is a simplified schematic of N.V. Philips, a Dutch multinational company. The size of the nodes, or circles, in the figure indicate the size and relative importance of the SBU it represents. Interestingly, the circle is larger for the United States than it is

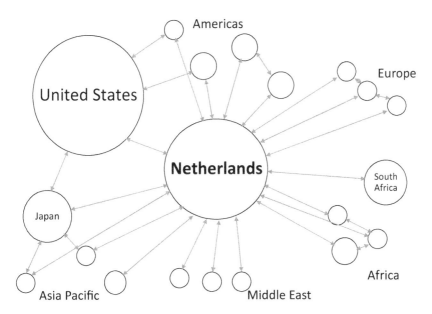

Figure 8.7 Transnational network structure example of N.V. Philips

for the headquarters in the Netherlands. This is an indication that, within a global firm and under certain situations, subsidiaries might demand (and receive) more freedom and control than others, discussed later. Despite being a Dutch company from the Netherlands, the American market is very important to the overall corporation. However, note that the connections in and out of the Netherlands are the most numerous. Arrows represent communications between business units. Most of the subsidiary connections are at the regional level—e.g., Asian and Oceania countries in the Asia Pacific region are linked at the bottom left and American countries (both North and South) are more linked with each other at the top of the network. Most of the Middle Eastern subsidiaries do not appear to communicate with one another but directly with the Netherlands HQ, perhaps an indication of the political discord and multiple cultural identities in the region. The seemingly distinct relationship with South Africa probably stems from the fact that South Africa was primarily a Dutch colony at one point—again demonstrating the importance of colonial history to business global practices.

Structure Follows Strategy

It is a famous truism that "structure follows strategy". Thus, we would expect that the structures that we utilize for our globalized organization should follow from the global strategy that we have chosen to pursue. Paralleling the integration–responsiveness framework of global strategic orientations, an organization's structural choices always involve two opposing forces: (1) the need for differentiation (i.e., focusing on and specializing in specific markets); and (2) the need for integration (i.e., coordinating functions used in those same markets). The way a firm is organized along the differentiation–integration continuum determines how well strategies, along the localization–globalization continuum, are implemented.

A globalization strategy treats the world as one market by using a standardized approach to products and markets. It usually involves rationalization (that is, consolidation of production and other functions) and the development of strategic alliances (to do the things the organization does not do well). To achieve rationalization, managers in product-based firms must choose the manufacturing location for each product based on where the best combination of cost, quality and technology can be attained. This means that different parts and components are often produced in different countries and that product design and marketing are, essentially, the same in all markets. As such, differentiation and specialization in local markets are minimized.

Table 8.1 Structure follows strategy—and other contingencies

STRATEGY	TYPICAL STRUCTURE	COORDINATION	IMPORTANCE OF ORGANIZATIONAL CULTURE	IMPORTANCE OF NATIONAL CULTURE
Global standard	Global product	High	Important	Low
International	International division	Medium	Medium	Medium
Multidomestic	Global area	Low	Low	High
Transnational	Multinational matrix	Very high	Critical	High

Another risk associated with globalization is exposure to volatility from all corners of the globe.

Table 8.1 tabulates the different strategies and their associated organizational structures, along with the corresponding effects of coordination requirements and organizational culture, which will be discussed in more detail in the next section. Recall that the two major issues in choosing the structure and design of an organization are the opportunities and need for (1) globalization and (2) localization. Over time, the strategic orientation of the organization may change—usually progressing from a simple international strategy towards a global or multidomestic one and then, ultimately, transnational. As the company progresses through various stages from domestic to transnational, the organizational structure must be adapted to accommodate changes in relative focus on globalization versus localization, choosing a global product structure, a geographic area structure or perhaps a matrix form over time. The corresponding criticalities of both organizational and national culture are shown in Table 8.2. Again, one can see the potential difficulty of managing a transnational strategy via a matrix structure, which requires an active management of both organizational and national cultures.

A Note on Control Systems and Structures

The requirement for structure in matching strategy stems from the notion of control within an organization. From the area of organizational behavior, you have probably heard about the principal–agency problem in management—namely, how do we know that an agent (in the form of our global subsidiary manager) is acting in the best interests and goals of our organization? There are three main aspects of controlling behavior and decision-making in any

Table 8.2 Control systems and characteristics of global strategies

	Control system			
	OUTPUT	BUREAUCRATIC	DECISION-MAKING	CULTURAL
Formalization	High	High	Medium	Low
Specialization	Medium	High	Medium	Medium
Centralization	Low	High	High	Low
Typical strategic condition where used extensively	High integration	High integration	High integration	High integration; High responsiveness
Typical strategy condition where not used	High responsiveness	High responsiveness	High responsiveness	

organization, which help ensure that managers act in the best interest of the larger organization. These are via: (1) formalization—i.e., the use of defined structures and systems in decision-making, communicating and controlling; (2) specialization—i.e., assigning individuals to specific, well-defined tasks; and (3) centralization—i.e., where all important decisions are made at the top.

There are also four basic types of control systems. The use of each control systems varies based on the type of global organizational structure chosen such that control systems and structure are intertwined. Output control is based on allowing SBUs free rein on policies and procedures but demanding that they achieve a specific output, like a certain level of profit growth or sales output. This is useful to allow decentralization, such as in the global area division. Bureaucratic control is based on having specific rules and regulations that all SBUs must follow, corporate-wide. The need for integration increases the use of such controls—for example, in the international and global product divisions. Decision-making control is about the level of centralization required in the corporation, with highly centralized organizations having most decisions made at the top. Again, strategies that require heavy integration, like the product division structure, tend to use centralized decision-making. National responsiveness tends towards decentralized decision-making. Finally, cultural (also sometimes called input) control is evident in the hiring and development of appropriate people in the organization with values and beliefs that lead to self-control and focus on specific outputs, and decision-making processes with which every internal actor innately agrees. In other words, this is using culture to make sure things are done the way they should be (respecting the values and beliefs that underlie that culture).

Management Practices and Organizational Structures that Vary across Organizational and National Cultures

Research suggests six aspects/practices/factors of management that vary within organizations and across national cultures (Deresky, 2014). Figure 8.8 depicts the polar ends of these six aspects of management, which may differ across organizations and nations in terms of cultural and managerial preferences. When planning the management functions of a foreign subsidiary it is important to take these into account for the specific context in which you are working.

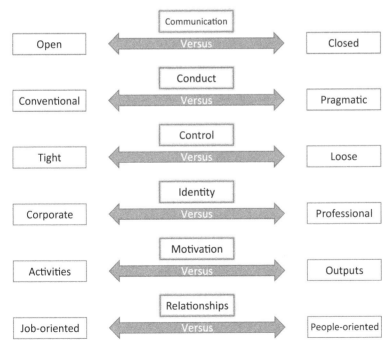

Figure 8.8 Six aspects of management

Source: Adapted from Deresky (2014)

We've already seen that different cultures may have different communication preferences. Additionally, some people from certain organizations and national cultures prefer to be motivated by the outputs of a process (e.g., producing a certain number of products) while others prefer to be motivated by the activities themselves (e.g., making sure the product is of high quality). Some organizations focus on the corporate culture and uphold the organizational values (e.g., "How we do things here …") rather than others who might pursue the ideals of their professional identities (e.g., "How we do things in my profession as a CPA"). Hence the poles of each management factor in Figure 8.8. You will want to explore the internet and/or using primary research for information on how the culture of the country you are analyzing tends to think about these factors and on which poles most peoples' preferences lie.

With these notions in mind (i.e., preferences for different managerial practices, etc.) and the emphasis on different foci, Fons Trompenaars developed a model of four types of organizational cultures that also maps to national cultures and their respective countries (see Hampden-Turner & Trompenaars, 1997). The model is useful for understanding the probability of success for mergers and acquisitions (M&As) involving organizations from different countries and cultural emphases.

Figure 8.9 depicts the four types of organizational cultures, which are based on the two continuums of (1) emphasis on the person versus the tasks and (2) emphasis on hierarchy versus equity. One should easily see the linkage to Hofstede's and GLOBE's national cultural dimensions, with hierarchy and person emphasis being associated with high power distance.

According to Trompenaars, there are four steps in the integration of organizational cultures resulting from international expansion via mergers/acquisitions. The two groups should (1) establish the purpose, goals and focus of the merger; (2) develop mechanisms to identify the most important structures and manager roles; (3) determine who has authority over resources; and (4) identify the expectations of all involved participants and facilitate communication between departments and individuals.

Figure 8.10 maps out various countries and where the typical "preferred" domestic organization fits into Trompenaars' model. Again, like the CAGE and other *cultural distance* analyses, organizations from countries that have similar organizational culture preferences will tend to be easier to integrate in mergers and acquisitions than will others in different quadrants. Specifically, we would expect the most failed M&As when linking organizations diagonally—when both continuums are mismatched. Moving up/down or sideways into a new quadrant would be better, because only one

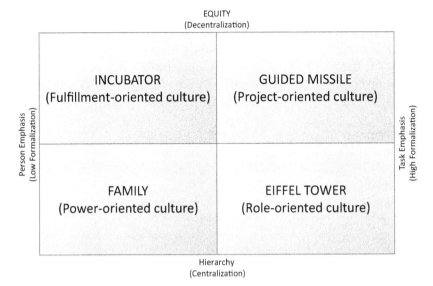

Figure 8.9 Trompenaars' model of national organizational culture

Source: Adapted from Hampden-Turner & Trompenaars (1997)

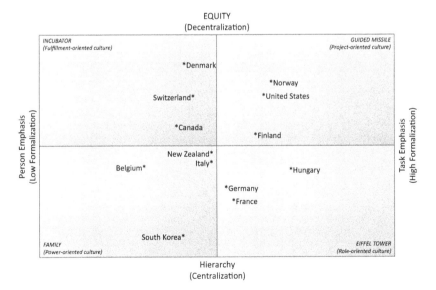

Figure 8.10 Countries applied to Trompenaars' model of national organizational culture

continuum is mismatched. Merging with companies within the same quadrant means that the basic organizational culture (at least, according to the model) remains matched, and therefore these M&As should have the highest probability of success among the different potential situations. This is useful when implementing the strategies of the upcoming chapters.

References

Deresky, H. (2014). *International management: Managing across borders and cultures: Text and cases* (7th ed.). New York: Prentice Hall.

Hampden-Turner, C., & Trompenaars, F. (1997). *Riding the waves of culture: Understanding diversity in global business.* New York: McGraw-Hill.

Mintzberg, H., & Van der Heyden, L. (1999). Organigraphs: Drawing how companies really work. *Harvard Business Review, 77*(5), 87–94.

Leadership, Motivation and Cross-Cultural Negotiation in the Global Context

9

Learning Objectives

By the end of this chapter, you will:

- Know the various leadership styles that are prevalent (used) or anathema (discouraged) in different parts of the world;
- Comprehend the link between cultural values and organizational members' motivation;
- Understand different negotiation styles and tactics and how they may differ in different parts of the world.

Practice Objectives

By the end of this chapter, you will be able to:

- Determine which leadership style is most appropriate for the cultural values of the region you are analyzing;
- Determine which motivational techniques might be most appropriate for the cultural values of the region you are analyzing;
- Create a strategy for negotiating a business deal that is most appropriate for the cultural and economic values and communication styles of the region you are analyzing.

What Is Leadership and Why Would It Differ across Nations?

Leadership is defined in the dictionary as "the action of leading a group of people or an organization", but this is a fairly tautological definition (i.e., "leadership is leading"!). It is more important for us to know when we can recognize leadership when we see it and what it is about leadership that makes it so important to strategy. As pointed out in earlier chapters, most strategy emanates from the top management of an organization, and this requires leadership. Even emergent or bottom-up strategic perspectives require leaders to ensure their success by appropriately resourcing the strategy's tactics and motivating the people in the organization towards implementing the strategy successfully. Recall, also, the importance of vision to strategy. All of this suggests that, without leadership, strategy cannot be successful.

To that extent, leading a group of people or an organization requires setting a vision for those people to follow and motivating a plan to achieve the vision. Recalling the House et al. (2004) definition is appropriate: Leadership is "the ability of an individual to influence, motivate, and enable others to contribute toward the effectiveness and success of the organizations of which they are members".

Before discussing how organizational members can be motivated, let's look at different types of leadership styles. In other words, we will examine ways in which top management can influence people. To begin, it is important to point out that managers are not necessarily leaders (and vice versa: leaders are not always from management). So, what distinguishes a leader from a manager? Some main differences include vision and motivation, mentioned above. Whereas managers can be good at getting things done, it is genuine leaders who pave new pathways to achieve things not yet known or enacted. Whereas managers earn respect by fiat (or the position that they occupy), leaders earn respect by their ability to inspire and the things that they do and achieve. Leaders often model the behaviors they wish to motivate.

We examine a few leadership models in this chapter, but in general a simple model of leadership-based managerial styles from across the globe is simply a model with three characteristics. This originally stems from William Ouchi's XYZ theory of managerial behavior, which states that managers chose to interact with their subordinates in one of three ways (Ouchi, 1981). Theory X states that managers essentially believe that people are basically lazy, and that coercion and threats of punishment are necessary to get them to work. Theory Y states that managers essentially believe that, under the right conditions, people not only will work hard but will seek increased responsibility and challenges. Theory Z states that managers essentially believe that workers seek opportunities to participate in management and are motivated by teamwork and responsibility sharing.

Theory XYZ correlates well with the three general leadership styles of authoritarian, paternalistic and participative. Authoritarian leaders use work-centered behavior designed to ensure task accomplishment (i.e., "Just do it, or else!")—essentially, by ordering people to do their jobs and firing them if they refuse. Paternalistic leaders use work-centered behavior as well but couple that with protective employee-centered concerns (i.e., "Do your job and I will take care of you"). Participative leaders use both work- and task-centered behavior and people-centered approaches to leading subordinates (i.e., "Do your job in ways that expand your horizons").

It becomes easy to see that cultures that are used to high power distance and dictator-based or authoritarian political regimes are more comfortable utilizing the authoritarian leadership style. Latin American countries, for example, are traditionally more authoritarian. However, there can be exceptions—e.g., leadership styles in Peru may be much closer to those in the United States than previously assumed.

Cultures where the father figure is an important cultural concept tend to be most comfortable with the paternalistic style of leadership. For example, Japan is well known for its paternalistic approach to leadership, and there is some evidence of this in China. Of course, the Chinese are becoming more participative or Westernized (from an authoritarian and paternalistic stance), but recent changes may be shifting back towards the authoritative stance. (Cultural norms do change but are also resilient and can reemerge over time.)

Democracies and cultures with low power distance are likely to be participative in nature. For example, European managers tend to use a participative leadership approach. Some evidence suggests a similarity between a Middle Eastern leadership style and those found in Western countries, although, once again, the recent shift in Saudi Arabia may be back towards an authoritative stance. Newly developing countries may be moving towards a more participative leadership style, to emulate the success of Western countries in terms of business. Some research suggests that participative styles may be most effective—as we'll see next.

Five Types of Leaders Based on Activeness

Bernard Bass' (1996) research on leadership traits of successful leaders suggested that a style he calls "transformational" is the most efficacious.

Transformational leaders (I) tend to be charismatic and enjoy the admiration of their followers. Bass identifies the four "I"s of this type of leader:

- Idealized influence
  - Enhancing pride, loyalty and confidence in their people; aligning followers by providing a common purpose or vision that the latter willingly accept.
- Inspirational motivation
  - Extremely effective in articulating vision, mission and beliefs in clear-cut ways.
- Intellectual stimulation
  - Able to get followers to question old paradigms and accept new views of the world.
- Individualized consideration
  - Able to diagnose and elevate the needs of each follower in a way that furthers each one's development.

The four other types of leadership are less effective than transformational. Contingent reward (CR) leaders clarify what needs to be done and provide psychic and material rewards to those who comply. CR leaders are the next most active and effective from I leaders. Active management-by-exception (MBE-A) leaders monitor their follower's performance and take corrective action when deviations from standards occur. Slightly more passive and less effective than MBE-As, Passive management-by-exception (MBE-P) leaders intervene in situations only when standards are not met. Finally, the most passive leaders, who lead by laissez-faire (LF), avoid intervening and do not accept responsibility for follower actions.

GLOBE Study's Six Types of Leadership Styles

Recall from Chapter 6 the GLOBE study, which identified six leadership characteristics, namely:

(1) Charismatic/value-based leadership, which reflects the ability to inspire, motivate and expect high performance outcomes from others based on firmly held core values.
(2) Team-oriented leadership, which emphasizes effective team building and the implementation of a common purpose or goal among team members.

Table 9.1 GLOBE measures on leadership for different countries

	Brazil	China	Denmark	India	Mexico	United States
Charisma	6.01	5.57	6.01	5.85	5.66	6.12
Team	6.17	5.57	5.70	5.72	5.75	5.80
Self-protective	3.50	3.80	2.82	3.78	3.86	3.16
Participative	6.06	5.05	5.80	4.99	4.64	5.93
Humane	4.84	5.18	4.23	5.26	4.71	5.21
Autonomous	2.27	4.07	3.79	3.85	3.86	3.75

Source: Data sourced at https://globeproject.com

(3) Participative leadership, which reflects the degree to which managers involve others in making and implementing decisions.
(4) Humane-oriented leadership, which reflects supportive and considerate leadership and includes compassion and generosity.
(5) Autonomous leadership, which refers to independent and individualistic leadership attributes.
(6) Self-protective leadership, which focuses on ensuring the safety and security of the individual and group through status enhancement and face saving.

As displayed in Table 9.1, the GLOBE study finds different values (with a scale from 1 to 7) for each of the six measures of leadership styles across the world. For example, the charismatic leadership style can be seen to be utilized quite clearly in the United States but less so in China. The opposite is the case for the self-protective and autonomous leadership styles, which are more prevalent in China than the United States. Exploring data from the GLOBE study online can help determine whether the leadership styles of the countries you are analyzing match up or not.

Leadership, Motivation and Differences across Cultures

Students of management are usually familiar with the theory of motivation by Abraham Maslow, which has been taught for decades in business schools. In general, Maslow's hierarchy of needs states that people are motivated to act depending upon where they stand regarding the satiation of needs that they currently have attained (Maslow, 1943). These needs are shown in the left part of the diagram in Figure 9.1. Thus, if one's physiological needs for food, water and basic survival needs is met, but not others, that individual will be motivated by concerns or needs for safety like shelter and

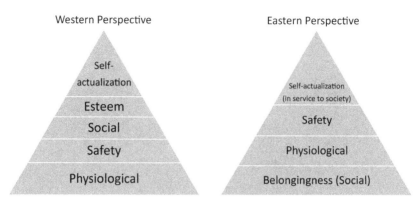

Figure 9.1 Maslow's hierarchy of needs in Western and Eastern contexts
Source: Adapted from Gambrel & Cianci (2003)

security. Over the years, critiques of Maslow's hierarchy have gained ground. Criticisms of Maslow's hierarchy include whether needs in the lower part of the hierarchy really need to be satisfied before one is interested in motivation towards higher-order needs. For our purposes, a major criticism of Maslow's hierarchy of needs is that it was developed in, and mostly applied to, the Western civilization context. Other parts of the world have been sometimes found to exhibit different orders of hierarchy and actual need (Gambrel & Cianci, 2003).

For example, as shown in the right-hand part of the diagram of Figure 9.1, Asian societies (particularly those based on Confucian philosophies) place a more important emphasis on belongingness or social needs—sometimes before their own physiological needs are met![1] Moreover, whereas self-actualization (the highest form of need and awareness) in the West is often seen as an individualization of the psyche (i.e., making oneself "satisfied" by sheer willpower), in the East self-actualization in interpreted in terms of one's service towards society.

Thus, different societies or levels of a cultural spectrum may exhibit different motivational effects. This was indeed found in a study by Geert Hofstede, which shows that the main motivators for lower-echelon employees were clearly focused on security and physiological needs, such as physical conditions of work and earnings. Middle managers were mostly motivated by a cooperative workplace and friendliness, which clearly centered on social needs. This all compared to high-level management and professionals, who tended to be motivated by needs for self-actualization via a challenging work-place with training, autonomy and use of up-to-date skills (Hofstede, 1972).

The connection with leadership should be clear. Leaders, if they are to influence people to move towards the visions they create, need to understand what motivates their followers. Furthermore, what motivates their followers will depend upon the culture and level of societal advancement for the specific individual.

Frederick Herzberg developed a model of motivation with which many management scholars are also familiar, and which is more closely tied to management practices (Herzberg, 1966). Figure 9.2 places the two major theories of motivation side by side to display the similarities. Herzberg talks about two main factors that influence motivation (hence the two-factor theory). Hygiene factors are aspects of a job that does not necessarily motivate employees to work harder but could demotivate employees if they were taken away or inadequate. Motivators are factors that will positively motivate employees to work harder if they are introduced or increased. Thus, workers expect certain safe working conditions that, if not present, cause dissatisfaction. Being given more responsibility for one's job has been shown to result in more productivity and worker motivation. As with Maslow's theory, different cultures may be motivated slightly differently (e.g., the working conditions expected in Vietnam may be different from those expected in the United States. This is certainly true of China, where the author has photographic evidence of a grandmother and child walking

Maslow's Model	*Herzberg's Model*
Self-actualization	Motivators-
	Achievement
	Recognition
Esteem	Responsibility
	Advancement
	The work itself
Social	Hygiene factors-
	Salary
	Technical Supervision
Safety	Company policies
	Interpersonal relationships
Physiological	Working conditions

Figure 9.2 Maslow's and Herzberg's theories compared

amongst a construction site without helmets! In China, at least at the time, construction workers often lived on-site with their families ...). As a culture or country gets used to better working conditions, these will be expected to continue to be offered to maintain the same level of motivation.

Negotiation across Cultures

Leadership and motivation are the topics of the chapter so far. Both these concepts tie into negotiation, given that the main tasks of negotiation are to influence the other bargaining party towards sharing your vision of a future business proposal. Thus, understanding the leadership traits and what motivates people in other cultures will be important to successfully negotiating contracts and solidifying business relationships throughout the world.

Figure 9.3 illustrates the general negotiation process, starting with preparation for talks and ending with agreement. The process remains similar throughout the world but may change in terms of when various sub-processes or stages are important or end. That is, in most Western cultures based on common or civil law, the end of negotiations and the beginning of a legal contract comes in the concessions and agreement stage. However, in many Asian

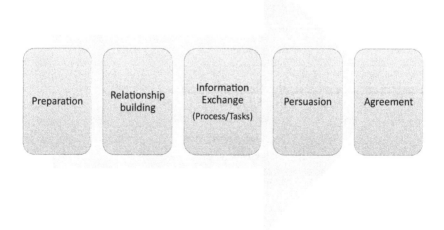

Figure 9.3 The general negotiation process

cultures the signing of the contract is only the beginning of the "give and take" of negotiations. Indeed, the relationship *is* the contract in most Chinese business situations. This comes as a shock to Western businesspeople, who focus on the legal aspects of a contract and see relationships as much more transactional. Other stages may be (more or less) important; or embedded throughout the entire process. Relationship building, following the comments here, can be considered an embedded aspect of the entire process in China, whereas in the United States it may be a small part of the process in the initial stages of negotiations.

As another example, Japan has a high-context and very risk-averse culture, and one can see these traits in the general choices made in the negotiation process. The team size tends to be large and the relationship-building stage is seen as very important and prolonged. While the top leader makes the final decision about agreement, general consensus building is emphasized through a process called *nemawashi*, which involves talking with organizational members and getting feedback on ideas and proposals. In the West this would be referred to as building the groundwork for negotiations, and it often follows a middle-down-top (think layers of management) flow of information in leading towards the finalization and agreement on a plan.

When creating a strategy towards negotiating in a new cultural setting you need to do as much research as possible about the cultural preferences of the other negotiating party. For instance, in some cultures only the top management team or leaders are considered negotiating partners. Sending junior staff in such cases can stop negotiations in its tracks. Using cultural and communication models from previous chapters combined with the notions of leadership styles and motivational factors that vary across cultures will help to enhance the probability of successful negotiations. In fact, it may change the very notion of what success means. For example, whereas in the past a signed contract might be the measure of success, the new measure might be the increased trust of and a better working relationship with a valuable business partner.

Note

1 If you take this to its logical conclusion, people are willing to starve to death before they allow themselves to be ostracized from their communities. While extreme, we sometimes see this in many cultures where religious beliefs of belongingness are strong—even in the West. For example, see examples of religious sects that refuse medical treatment based on religious doctrine.

References

Bass, B. M. (1996). Is there universality in the full range model of leadership? *International Journal of Public Administration, 19*(6), 731–761.

Gambrel, P. A., & Cianci, R. (2003). Maslow's hierarchy of needs: Does it apply in a collectivist culture? *Journal of Applied Management and Entrepreneurship, 8*(2), 143–161.

Herzberg, F. (1966). *Work and the nature of man*. Cleveland: World Publishing.

Hofstede, G. (1972). The colors of collars. *Columbia Journal of World Business, 7*(5), 72–80.

House, R. J., Hanges, P. J., Javidan, M., Dorfman, P. W., & Gupta, V. (eds.) (2004). *Culture, leadership, and organizations: The GLOBE study of 62 societies*. Thousand Oaks, CA: Sage.

Maslow, A. H. (1943). A theory of human motivation. *Psychological Review, 50*(4), 370–96.

Ouchi, W. G. (1981). *Theory Z: How American business can meet the Japanese challenge*. New York: Avon Books.

Managing People in the Global Context

10

Learning Objectives

By the end of this chapter, you will:

- Know the human resource issues (including selection, training and development) to be managed within the successful globalized organization for the international setting;
- Comprehend the link between HR practices and organizational members' motivations and successes, which transfers to the success of the globalized organization;
- Understand how approaches to different HR issues may differ in different parts of the world;
- Know the types of managers that can be employed by a global organization (e.g., expatriates, home-based, trans-pats, etc.) and the effects that choice of management type has on successful globalization.

Practice Objectives

By the end of this chapter, you will be able to:

- Determine which type of subsidiary manager is most appropriate for the cultural values of the region you are analyzing;
- Determine which HR issues need to be addressed for the cultural values of the region you are analyzing;

- Create a strategy for staffing a foreign subsidiary that is most appropriate for the cultural values of the region you are analyzing.

Characteristics of Managers/Workers for International Assignments

It takes a special individual to be able to work in an environment that is culturally different from the one in which he or she is familiar. It also takes a special individual to withstand the stresses and uncertainties associated with international travel and work. While international assignments can be lucrative and exciting, they can also be costly in terms of work effort, health tolls and pressures on family life. If you are thinking about partaking in international work, it will help to have the following traits.

People who are international workers are adaptable and independent. They tend to be self-reliant but not afraid of requesting help when needed. Due to stresses from new environments and situations that often need patience and energy (like going through immigration checkpoints and traveling 16 hours in a plane), they need to be physically and emotionally healthy. Age can be a factor, with younger people (sometime before having a family and kids) often being attracted to such hectic but exhilarating lifestyles. When they do have a family, the support offered by the organization towards the spouse and children is just as important as the support for the globalized workers themselves.

The more experienced and educated they are on cultural matters, the more successful international workers tend to be. Knowledge of the local language(s) is often required, especially for a more complete integration in the cultural milieu. However, English speakers can often get by, as it is the *lingua franca* of modern global business.[1] Ultimately, global workers tend to be leaders in their field and motivated by the work itself—looking for adventure and excitement in both their work and leisure times.

Coming back home from a long-term assignment abroad has its own challenges too. Often, returning expats find that their new assignments seem less challenging and rewarding than their international work. While compatriots at the home office might have been promoted through various ranks, they may find themselves having to backtrack to a position similar to the one they were in when they first accepted the international assignment. Culture shock (which we look at later) in reverse may become an issue. Global managers and workers, as well as the HR department of the larger organization, need to take these factors into account for successful repatriation of the returning expat.

Staffing Approaches for Global Operations

Organizations filling managerial positions in the globalized environment can utilize one or more of four staffing approaches: (1) ethnocentric, (2) polycentric, (3) region-centric; and (4) global or transnational. The ethnocentric approach employs key managerial positions with people from the organization's domestic headquarters. These types of assigned individuals are named parent-country nationals (PCNs)—or sometimes referred to as home-country nationals or expatriates (namely expats). The advantages of this approach include PCN familiarity with the home organization's goals, products, technology, policies and procedures. The approach can also deal with issues of inadequate local managerial skills and the need to maintain close control on practices and policies. Some disadvantages are the lack of opportunities and development for local managers, resulting in poor adaptation and the lack of effectiveness of expatriates in foreign countries. This approach also can perpetuate ineffective home-country processes and prevent the company from taking advantage of the worldwide pool of management skill.

The polycentric staffing approach is often used with a multinational strategy. It employs key positions with host-country nationals (HCNs). HCNs are local managers hired to fill key positions in their own country. This approach helps companies to "act local". It can be less expensive than using PCNs and can help with managing problems in sensitive political situations. Often this approach is achieved by first acquiring foreign firms and retaining their management staff. Disadvantages of the polycentric approach include difficulty coordinating activities and goals between the subsidiary and parent company and conflicting loyalties for local managers. In addition, not sending headquarters' managers means that they do not gain overseas experience, which would help spread organizational values and practices from headquarters itself.

The global staffing approach uses the best managers recruited from either within the organization or from outside, regardless of nationality. Such individuals are often called third-country nationals (TCNs). Advantages of this approach include providing a greater pool of qualified and willing applicants from which to choose, which can further develop a cadre of global executives for the organization. Additionally, TCNs tend to be more culturally flexible and often speak two or more languages. They can be viewed as an acceptable compromise between headquarters versus local managers. It also can be more cost-effective to transfer and pay managers from some countries than from others, because their pay scale and benefits packages are lower.

As some individuals become truly global and move away from the concepts of host and home country, the term "transpatriate" is replacing the term "expatriate". Transpatriates can easily adapt to a number of different cultures in a dynamic way. However, implementing a global staffing approach is easier said than done, as there can be difficulty in finding high-quality mangers who are willing to transfer frequently around the world.

With the region-centric approach, recruiting, as the name suggests, is done on a regional basis. This approach can produce a mix of PCNs, HCNs and TCNs depending on the needs of the company or the product strategy. So, for example, a Chinese manager might be chosen to run a Thai outpost for a German company.

Here are overviews of these "types" of global managers based on where they originated. **Home-country nationals** are expatriate managers who are citizens of the country where the multinational organization is headquartered. The most common reason for using home-country nationals is to get the overseas operation under way. **Host-country nationals** are local managers hired by the MNC who are familiar with the culture and know the local language. They are less expensive than home-country personnel, and hiring them can make for good public relations in the foreign market. **Third-country nationals** are managers who are citizens of countries other than the country in which the MNC is headquartered or the one in which the managers are assigned to work by the MNC. These people have the necessary expertise for the job. **Inpatriates** (also sometimes called "inpats") are individuals from a host country or a third-country national who are assigned to work in the home country. The use of inpatriates recognizes the need for diversity at the domestic office and can help organizations better develop their global core competences. Companies can subcontract or outsource inpats to take advantage of lower human resource costs and increase their flexibility.

Success Factors and the Process of Adapting to New Cultural Settings

An important responsibility of international human resource (IHR) managers is that of managing expatriates and their development. Most multinationals underestimate the importance of the human resource planning function in the selection, training, acculturation and evaluation of expatriates.

As pointed out earlier, it takes a special person to be a successful expat. Although there are many factors that contribute to expatriate success, many IHR personnel directors select expatriates based on their domestic track records and technical expertise, without regard to the traits mentioned earlier. The need to ascertain whether potential expatriates have the necessary cross-cultural awareness and interpersonal skills is often overlooked. Studies suggest there are five categories of success for expatriates.

(1) **Job factors**, which relate to technical expertise (while the other four are more based on the actual personality of the candidate).
(2) **Relational dimensions** refer to the ability to relate to other people and sensitive situations.
(3) The **motivation state** is the attitude towards situations. Being "gung-ho" or excited about one's assignment helps.
(4) **Family considerations** are paramount. An unhappy spouse can be a deal breaker for overseas assignments, and this is often overlooked (to the peril of management).
(5) **Language skills** are, ultimately, important.

Determining whether the expatriate will be successful using these five dimensions can be challenging. Research indicates that extroverted managers with a high tolerance for stress are more likely to adjust to overseas assignments and perform well (McCormick & Chapman, 1996).

A study by R. J. Stone (1991) compares the importance of ten factors for either Australian, Asian or expat managers. The ability to personally adapt is in the top two for all managers, and for the family to adapt is in the top three. This is especially important for the Asian managers; they rated it more important than technical competence! In general, the ranking seems to follow this order (with the first being most important): (1) ability to adapt; (2) technical competence; (3) spouse/family adaptability; (4) human resource skills; (5) desire to do overseas work; (6) previous overseas experience; (7) host-country cultural knowledge; (8) academic qualifications; (9) host-country language abilities; and (10) home-country cultural knowledge.

Culture Shock and the Process for Adjusting to It

Figure 10.1 shows the typical movement in perceived competence over time when entering a new cultural environment. Note that, after an initial drop, there is often a feeling of "fantasia": That one knows all that is needed for managing within the new culture (due to one's previous studying and preparation for the assignment, etc.). Inevitably, there is a sudden drop in perceived competence when people realize that they do not fully comprehend the new

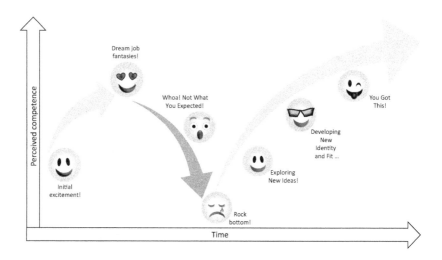

Position in Timeline of Figure Above	Stage	Perspective of the Expat
😊	*Unreality*	• A sense that the relocation is dream-like
😍	*Fantasia*	• Further enchantment and excitement with the new environment and a sense of Fantasy
😮	*Interest*	• Reality begins to "creep in" that the new environment is not the same as one's home
		POTENTIAL END OF RELOCATION
😣	*Acceptance of Reality*	• Conscience evaluation that the environment is different and that the Expat wants to continue
😃	*Experimentation*	• Testing new approaches to the environment and getting cultural feedback
😎	*Search*	• Looking for meaning in behaviors and attitudes and developing new models and personal theories to cope
😉	*Integration*	• Final acceptance of the new environment and integrating one's behavior to fit in it

Figure 10.1 Perceived competence over time for overseas or new culture assignments
Source: McCormick & Chapman (1996: 368)

culture. We often refer to this sudden awareness as "culture shock": a state of disorientation and anxiety about not knowing how to behave in an unfamiliar culture. If it is not corrected, this may result in the end of the assignment and a return to one's home culture. However, global workers who are able to overcome the "shock" can enter the stage of acceptance, and begin the real learning process via experimentation and the searching for deeper meanings needed for true integration into the culture. Now you can see the need for the personality traits mentioned earlier! While someone may never be fully immersed in the deep structures of the new culture, by following the process of Figure 10.1 both perceived and real competence will increase to the point that the global worker becomes a functional participant in the new environment. In other words, cultural empathy can lead towards cultural adaptability …

To help with this process one should anticipate an adjustment period. Training and previous experience before the new assignment can help speed up the process towards real competence in the new culture. Some in-country adjustment time needs to be planned for as part of the process. Some important aspects are the individual's ability to adjust effectively and to maintain a positive outlook. Interacting well with host nationals to perceive and evaluate the host-country's cultural values and norms correctly is paramount.

One goal of cross-cultural training is to reduce culture shock. The cause of culture shock is the trauma people experience in new cultures, when they lose the familiar signs and cues that they had previously used to interact in daily life and when they must learn to cope with new cues and expectations. Results or symptoms of culture shock include the inability to work effectively, family stress and hostility towards host nationals. Culture shock (seen in the dip in Figure 10.1) usually progresses through four general stages:

(1) The honeymoon phase includes positive attitudes and excitement and may last up to several weeks.
(2) The irritation/hostility phase is the crisis stage, when cultural differences result in problems at home and work. It is characterized by homesickness, and many expatriates never get past this phase.
(3) Gradual adjustment is a phase of recovery, in which the expatriate begins to understand and predict patterns of behavior, interact with others in the host-country language and accept his or her new life.
(4) Biculturalism is the stage in which the expatriate and family members grow to accept and appreciate local people and practices and are able to function effectively in two cultures. Many people never get to this stage, but operate acceptably at the third stage.

Finally, there exists a concept called subculture shock as well. It occurs when a manager is transferred to another part of his or her own country where there are cultural differences—essentially, from what he or she perceives to be a "majority" culture to a "minority" one. The shock comes from feeling like an "immigrant" in one's own country and being unprepared for such differences. So, the lesson of international human resource management (IHRM) can also apply to some domestic HR transfer situations.

Compensation Schemes for Staffing Global Operations

Compensating expatriates can be difficult, because there are many variables to consider.

Most compensation packages are designed around four common elements: (1) base salary, (2) allowances, (3) benefits and (4) taxes.

The base salary is the amount of money that an expatriate normally receives in the home country. However, normally employees need allowances and other benefits (such as a bonus) to entice them to travel and live abroad. The awarding of benefits will create many questions:

- Should host-country legislation regarding termination of employment affect employee benefits entitlements?
- Is the home or host country responsible for the expatriates' social security benefits?
- Should benefits be subject to the requirements of the home or host country?
- Which country should pay for the benefits?
- Should other benefits be used to offset any shortfall in coverage?
- Should home-country benefit programs be available to local nationals?
- How should any double-taxation issues be handled?
- Etc.

Allowances are payments made to entice employees to work abroad and offset the costs (real and opportunity-based) associated with international expatriate work. A cost-of-living allowance is payment for differences between the home country and the overseas assignment. These are designed to provide the expatriate the same standard of living enjoyed in the home country. They may cover a variety of expenses, including relocation, housing, education and hardship.

Other benefits may be added to entice the best managers to go abroad. As part of their benefits package, a growing number of organizations have replaced the ongoing premium for overseas assignments with a one-time, lump-sum bonus.

Finally, taxes become a big issue for expatriate workers, especially from the United States, which requires its citizens to report and pay taxes on all worldwide income. Tax equalization—whereby the worker pays the taxes he or she would have paid in the home country—is important. An expatriate may have two tax bills for the same income unless a tax treaty exists between the two countries. The globalized organization usually pays the extra tax burden, as otherwise this would be a negative incentive.

International Human Resource Management Practices and the Effects of Varying Cultures and Legal Environments

Table 10.1 lists the five major practices or responsibilities associated with HR and the important legal and cultural aspects that might affect these practices. Depending on the chosen location in the world, the subsidiary will need to independently manage these different HR preferences (Sparrow & Budhwar,

Table 10.1 Five HR practices and differences across legal and cultural environments

HR PRACTICE/ RESPONSIBILITY	*CULTURAL NORMS*	*LEGAL ISSUES*
Recruitment and selection	Individualism/collectivism	Nepotism laws
	Masculinity	Equal pay/gender issues
		Requirements for hiring locals
Training and development	Time orientation	Certification/training requirements
		Location of training (HQ versus local)
	Apprenticeship Tendencies	Type of education (school versus on the job)
Performance appraisal	Power distance	Seniority issues
	Status	Local standards of performance
	Privacy issues	
	Face-saving tendencies	
Compensation	Uncertainty avoidance	Local standards of compensation
	Loyalty and harmony	Group versus individual compensation
		Unemployment compensation plans
Labor relations	Work attitudes	Local labor laws
	Union propensity	Union power
	Loyalty and harmony	Governance structure (e.g., co-determination in Germany)
	Paternalism	Collective bargaining rights

1997). One needs to carefully explore the connections in the cultures that one is thinking of entering as part of an organization's global strategy.

Careful analysis of the cultural and legal environment for specific countries is necessary to make the correct decision for each practice. For example, the recruitment and selection of new employees may be affected by the cultural factor of individualism and employment laws. In collectivist societies that allow for the hiring of friends and family, without regard for the public good, issues of nepotism (which is illegal in many countries) may be prevalent.

Cultures with long-term orientations highly value training and development. However, in some countries, attitudes and practices towards training and development differ. For example, apprenticeships are more common in Germany than in the United States, and in China training is mandated by some government policies for companies that want to enter the country. Whether training should be done in the home or host country needs to be determined based on the type of knowledge being transferred and other legal aspects of the situation.

The performance appraisal practices will differ across cultures based on such aspects as power distance and the traditional ways of evaluating people and work. Cultures with high power distance will be more tolerant of a strict boss–subordinate relationship. Traditions may influence processes, such as in Japan, where seniority rather than performance itself can determine who gets a promotion. In cultures where saving face is important, such as in China, it can be difficult to be frank in appraisal conversations, etc.

The legal system will heavily influence the compensation practices but cultural issues of uncertainty avoidance and group versus individual appraisals can influence payment packages. For example, in cultures where harmony is important, often group pay is emphasized versus individual compensation based on individual performance.

Finally, labor relations will also depend on legal and cultural environments. For example, in some countries and cultures, labor unions are widely accepted and need to be part of the negotiation process when entering a new country. In Germany, for instance, the concept of "co-determination"—in which union members are required to sit on the board of German companies—is law.

Again, as with other aspects of managing the global strategy, HR specialists, lawyers and accountants must be consulted about the specific issues for the country being analyzed. Each situation will be unique. This book should give you a start in exploring those specific situations.

Note

1 I often tell my students that an unfortunate side effect of English as the global language of business is that if they, as primarily English-speaking people, want to practice a second language it is often hard to find others to practice with unless they are already fluent in the other language. Most will just automatically speak back to you in English!

References

McCormick, I., & Chapman, T. (1996). Executive relocation: Personal and organizational tactics. In Warner, M., & Joynt, P. (eds.), *Managing across cultures: Issues and perspectives* (pp. 326–337). London: International Business Press.

Sparrow, P. R., & Budhwar, P. S. (1997). Competition and change: Mapping the Indian HRM recipe against world-wide patterns. *Journal of World Business, 32*(3), 224–242.

Stone, R. J. (1991). Expatriate selection and failure. *Human Resource Planning, 14*(1), 9–18.

Managing Foreign Market Entry

11

Learning Objectives

By the end of this chapter, you will:

- Know the various modes of market entry;
- Comprehend the link between market entry modes and the cultural and PESTEL aspects of the country to be entered;
- Understand the issues involved in the different market entry modes and how they may differ in different parts of the world.

Practice Objectives

By the end of this chapter, you will be able to:

- Determine which type of market entry mode is most appropriate for the mix of organizational values and cultural values as well as the legal/business environment of the region you are analyzing;
- Create a strategy for your foreign subsidiary's market entry mode that is most appropriate for the mix of organizational values and cultural values of the region and country you are analyzing.

Business and Corporate Strategy

Most of what we have discussed about strategy so far in this book has had to do with business strategy. That is, we've focused on how a single organization should compete in order to give itself a competitive advantage over its rivals. (Again, this is true of non-profit organizations, as they also compete for resources and "customers"—e.g., donors—with other organizations in their non-profit industries!) However, most companies, particularly global ones, tend to be involved in multiple businesses. Many global non-profit organizations, like the International Red Cross and Red Crescent Movement, have, essentially, many different subsidiaries; so even they can be thought to have many organizations within a larger corporate umbrella. Indeed, corporate strategy is the strategic level of analysis in which we must ask ourselves what different businesses we should own or ally with. This is important with regard to global strategy, because often our efforts towards globalization result in either strategic alliances with other organizations or the merging with and/or acquisition of other organizations.

Corporate strategy is about answering the build, borrow or buy question; that is, in entering a new business and market, should we build our own new business, ally with another company or buy one? In fact, this major question is one of the last strategic questions we need to answer when going global before getting into the hard job of *actually* implementing the operations of our foreign efforts. Answering it will depend on the internal resources and capabilities we already have and the external factors, including cultural and legal aspects, of the environment we will enter.

The next, final two chapters focus on these issues. Here we discuss subjects revolving around the mode of entry, or "vehicle", by which we will enter the new foreign market of our choosing. The last chapter of the book examines the special cases of working closely with other organizations by either allying with them or buying them outright.

Two sets of considerations drive the location of foreign entries: (1) strategic goals and (2) cultural and institutional distances. Refer back to the CAGE model for the latter considerations. We'll look at the first considerations here as reasons to explore foreign market entry modes. In particular, the reasoning behind foreign market entry is that certain locations possess geographical features that are difficult for others to match, which results in location-specific advantages. "Agglomeration economies" is the term used to describe the benefits that accumulate when firms and people locate near one another together in cities and industrial clusters and create location-specific advantages that occur when there are a number of economic activities in a particular locality. These types of location-specific advantages may stem from (1) knowledge spillovers among closely located firms, (2) industry demand that creates a skilled labor force or (3) industry demand that facilitates a pool of specialized suppliers and buyers. Agglomeration thus explains why certain cities and regions can attract businesses even in the absence of obvious geographic advantages.

Table 11.1 Strategic goals and location-specific advantages

STRATEGIC FOCUS	INDUSTRY/COUNTRY EXAMPLES
Natural resources	Mining/oil resources in Canada, Australia or the Middle East
Markets	Consumer goods in large market countries like China and India
Efficiency	Manufacturing in China, Vietnam and other low-cost/high-worker-quality countries
Innovation	Information technology in India and Silicon Valley, United States; biotech in Boston and Singapore

It is important to match a firm's strategic goals to potential locations for entry. As alluded to in Chapter 1, four generic strategic goals will drive the decision to enter a particular foreign market. These are: (1) (natural) resource-seeking goals, whereby organizations go to specific locations to access specific resources; (2) market-seeking goals, whereby organizations go to countries that have a high demand for their products and services; (3) efficiency-seeking goals, whereby organizations single out the most efficient locations featuring a combination of scale economies and low-cost factors, including agglomeration; and (4) innovation-seeking goals, whereby organizations target countries and regions renowned for generating world-class innovations (Peng, 2016). Note that these last two are also resource-seeking behaviors. Also note that, while these four generic strategic goals are analytically distinct, they are not mutually exclusive such that an organization can enter a new country to achieve more than one type of strategic goal at a time. Table 11.1 lists some examples of each goal-seeking behavior.

Modes of Entry

After deciding which country to enter, management needs to think about the method used to enter the foreign market. This is called the "mode of entry". The choice of the mode and the scale of entry is important to the overall strategic commitment and management of the globalization effort. There are various modes of entry that are possible, starting with the least committed and smallest in scale of an import-export position and continuing downwards to the most committed (in terms of resources) and largest investment, which is the fully owned or wholly owned subsidiary. The amount of resources committed to entering a foreign market is determined by the choice of entry mode. Large-scale entries show a strategic commitment to certain markets and assure local customers and suppliers that the company is in the country for the long run. They might also deter potential entrants if industry capacity and other barriers to entry are in place before competitors can also enter the foreign market. However, these types of large-scale entry mode create hard-to-reverse strategic commitments that can limited strategic flexibility. Huge losses can occur if the large-scale bets are wrong.

Small-scale entries provide for real option strategies in which small investments can allow an organization to still be in the market without limiting the flexibility to increase the investment at a later date when more information is known about the probability of success for the venture. Thus, small scale entries are less expensive and can limit the downside risk of foreign entry in the initial exploratory stages of a global strategy. They allow for focus on organization learning. However, they may lead to a lack of the commitment necessary to build market share and capture first-mover advantages. As such, a careful balance must be made between the need to commit adequate resources towards successful entry and the flexibility to have other options in the case of failure.

Entry modes can be expressed as either non-equity or equity-based (Pan & Tse, 2000). Non-equity modes of entering foreign markets involve contracting without ownership commitments by the globalizing organization, usually through exports and/or contractual agreements (i.e., arm's-length transactions). They tend to reflect relatively small commitments to foreign markets. Equity modes of entering foreign markets may take place via joint ventures (JVs) and/or wholly owned subsidiaries (WOSs)—sometimes referred to as wholly foreign-owned enterprises or wholly owned foreign enterprises (WFOEs or WOFEs) and pronounced as "wolfies". They indicate a somewhat larger, hard-to-reverse commitment and the establishment of independent organizations in host countries.

Figure 11.1 categorizes the entry mode choices by whether they are equity-based or not. The realm of strategic alliances is within the large box and represents modes that use carefully aligned long-term relationships with partners already in or familiar with the foreign market. Direct exporting is a basic mode of entry that capitalizes on economies of, scale in production concentrated in the home country and selling directly into the foreign country. Indirect exporting uses a domestically based export intermediary to sell in the foreign market. In these cases, business is done on a transactional basis only—i.e., goods change hands via seller–buyer transactions. The other non-equity modes are contractual in nature but longer in term and thus strategic. Licensing/franchising agreements have the licensor/franchisor sell the rights of an intellectual property or a business model to a licensee/franchisee for a royalty fee. Turnkey projects happen when a client pays contractors to

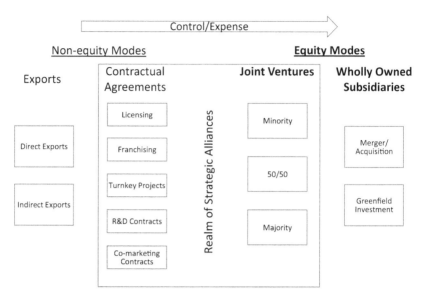

Figure 11.1 Entry mode choices

design and construct new facilities and train personnel for the organization. Specifically, a build–operate–transfer (BOT) agreement involves building and operating a facility for a period of time before transferring operations to a domestic agency or firm. Research and development contracts are outsourcing agreements between firms whereby one conducts R&D for the other. Co-marketing comprises efforts among a number of firms to jointly market their products and services.

Equity modes are used to establish a longer-term presence. Joint ventures are new corporate entities jointly created and owned by two or more parent companies. Wholly owned subsidiaries are subsidiaries located in a foreign country that are entirely owned by the parent organization. When creating a WOS the organization can choose to build new factories and offices from scratch—called greenfield operations—or acquire an existing organization already in the foreign market.

As seen at the top of Figure 11.1, control and expenses increase as one moves towards the use of equity modes of entry. Figure 11.2 depicts the tradeoff between the risks of utilizing a particular entry mode and the reward delivered in the form of managerial control. That is, lower forms of entry like exporting expose the organization to low risk (i.e., you can easily change an export contract or back out without losing a big investment), but such modes provide little control to the organization and do not show commitment to

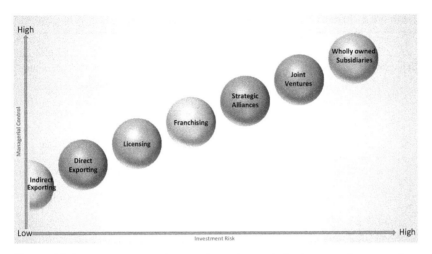

Figure 11.2 Risk versus reward (ownership and control) for the types of entry modes

the foreign market that foreign stakeholders like the local government might want. Heavier investment options like WOSs may expose the organization to huge investment risks, but ownership of the foreign assets and resources means that the organization can make whatever changes or accommodations it wants within legal and ethical boundaries. Thus, higher investments bring higher risks but also more control for the organization. This control issue will be more important, the more that things such as quality and brand reputation are important to the organization (see the Colgate case below).

Table 11.2 list the advantages and disadvantage of each type of entry mode. When deciding which mode to utilize the organization should consider the amount of risk exposure it is willing to take on and the need for managerial control. This may depend on the PESTEL and CAGE analyses that have been conducted on the foreign market already. That is, some countries might pose a higher risk of asset expropriation (i.e., the government seizing one's property), which makes equity-based modes potentially more dangerous. On the other hand, some countries require certain modes as the basis for allowing market entry in the first place. For example, in the past China has required the use of JVs to enter its large consumer market, making the commitment to entering China highly risky. Even with some types of entry mode that allow some control, careful understanding of the relationship is important. So, once again, the cultural, legal and political aspects of the country being contemplated needs to be considered when deciding on the most appropriate entry mode.

Table 11.2 Pros and cons of each market entry mode

		PROS	CONS
Exporting	*Direct*	Take advantage of domestic capacity and economies of scale	Lack of exporting country knowledge
		Manage distribution through direct control	Transportation costs (weight/value tradeoffs)
		Potential to learn more about new local market	Susceptible to protectionism and trade barriers
	Indirect	Take advantage of domestic capacity and economies of scale	Control over distribution hindered
		Utilize agent with local market knowledge	No potential to learn about new market
Contractual	*Licensing*	Low risk and costs	Potential for IP infringements
agreements			Little control possible
	Franchising	Low risk and costs	Potential for contractual issues
		Transfer business model	Potential control issues/need for local responsiveness
			Creation of knock-offs/competitors
	Turnkey projects	Enter countries where FDI is restricted	Security, corporate espionage issues
			Creation of more efficient competitors
			No long-term sustainable opportunity
	R&D contracts	Choosing best locations for knowledge sourcing	Potential for IP infringements
			Little control possible
			Creation of innovative competitors
			Security, corporate espionage issues
	Co-marketing	Leverage partners' customers	Heavy resources needed in coordination
	Contracts		

(continued)

Table 11.2 Cont.

		PROS	CONS
Equity modes	*Joint ventures*	Sharing costs and risks with partner(s)	Limited equity; share in profits
		Access to partners' knowledge and assets	Limited control; some risk of knowledge expropriation
		Seen as politically acceptable in many cases	Potential for divergence in interests of partners
	Acquisitions	Quick entry	Potential inter-organizational culture and business integration issues
		Leverage existing local market knowledge	Expensive (targets are often overbid in excess of value)
	Greenfield projects	Full control over operations	High costs
		Retain all profits	Requirement to learn new market alone
			Potential political risks

Note: FDI = foreign direct investment.

Colgate's acquisition of Hawley and Hazel (H&H) in China and its Darlie toothpaste is a case in point. When the large US toothpaste and consumer products company bought H&H it did not consider the reaction that US and other customers outside China would have towards the sale of the toothpaste that was once called "Darkie" and pictured a man in blackface on the package. Despite not being for sale in the United States, a boycott of Colgate products was started by some outraged US consumers. Eventually Colgate management tried to get rid of the brand, but it was a highly successful product in China itself and H&H did not want to change it. Unfortunately, in the negotiations for the acquisition of H&H, H&H maintained the managerial rights on its products and refused to get rid of the brand. Eventually the name was changed and the packaging updated to be less offensive, but the new "Darlie" toothpaste remains for sale, much to Colgate's embarrassment. The Chinese name of the brand is still written as 黑人牙膏 (*hēirén yágāo*), which in English translates to "Black Man Toothpaste". In fact, upon making the English name change, H&H utilized a Chinese-language advertising campaign that reassured customers that "Black Man Toothpaste is still Black Man

Toothpaste". An internet search will lead you to some examples of this mistake in branding.

The racist undertones of the brand are obvious to anyone from the United States and are potentially brand-shattering in the West, where such blatant racism is not tolerated. Obviously, some cultures are more (or less) tolerant of issues that may be considered highly insensitive in others. Being able to correct for these transgressions is necessary for successful global brand management. For Colgate, being able to distance itself from the H&H brand is important (note that there is no label with the Colgate brand on the packaging of Darlie), but just being associated with the H&H brand was, and can be, problematic. Thus, careful negotiation of managerial rights is needed when partnering a foreign strategic alliance. We discuss this topic in the next, and final, chapter.

References

Pan, Y., & Tse, D. (2000). The hierarchical model of market entry modes. *Journal of International Business Studies, 31*(4), 535–554.

Peng, M. (2016). *GLOBAL3*. New York: Cengage Learning.

Managing Alliances and Acquisitions

12

Learning Objectives

By the end of this chapter, you will:

- Know the differences between acquisitions and mergers and the internal and external factors that favor them over strategic alliances or a build strategy;
- Comprehend the links between managerial control, cultural and administrative factors in the foreign market and the choice of borrow or buy;
- Understand how approaches to the borrow or buy decision may differ in different parts of the world.

Practice Objectives

By the end of this chapter, you will be able to:

- Determine which type of borrow or buy decision is most appropriate based on the organization's internal strengths and weaknesses and the administrative, legal and cultural values of the region you are analyzing;
- Determine the imperative issues that need to be addressed in implementing a foreign market entry strategy for the region you are analyzing;
- Create a strategy for implementing a foreign market entry strategy for the region you are analyzing.

The Borrow or Buy Strategy when Entering a New Foreign Market

Continuing on the build, borrow or buy question from the last chapter, we now focus on the borrowing and buying of resources and capabilities necessary to enter a new foreign market. That is, we might use entry strategies of either working with another existing entity in a strategic alliance (borrowing) or outright buying or merging with one (buying). This is an important topic, because quite often it is impossible or inappropriate to build from scratch a foreign operation on one's own due to legal, cultural and economic issues that the new entrant may not really understand about the foreign market it is entering. Thus, even in cases of eventually building new operations in the foreign market, an organization might use the BOT (build–operate–transfer) strategy mentioned in Chapter 11 to get the process started successfully before the newcomer takes over. This is an example of a temporary strategic alliance based on a non-equity mode.

When an organization uses the buy strategy it purchases or merges with another existing entity. This is often referred to as a mergers and acquisitions strategy. Mergers are the combination of the operations and management of two firms to establish a new legal entity. Acquisition is the transfer of the control of operations and management from one firm to another, with the former becoming a unit of the latter. Although the term M&As is often used, in reality acquisitions dominate, and only a small percentage of M&As are truly mergers—with a genuine consolidation of equals.

Why Implement a Borrow or Buy Strategy when Entering a New Foreign Market?

Two perspectives (ultimately based on external and internal factors) are used to determine the reasoning behind the need and use of the borrow or buy strategies of alliances and acquisitions.

The institution-based view argues that institutions influence how a firm chooses between alliances and acquisitions. These institutions may be formally or informally based. The impact of formal institutions on alliances and acquisitions can be found along two dimensions: (1) antitrust concerns and (2) entry mode requirements. That is, governments of foreign countries may impose restrictions on acquisitions due to antitrust issues or they may require certain modes or vehicles as a precondition for market entry into their country's economy. This was the case, as mentioned earlier, in China and its requirement for foreign entities to utilize joint ventures when entering the Chinese market. With antitrust concerns, authorities favor alliances more than acquisitions. With entry mode requirements, certain governments limit the formation of acquisitions with foreign firms and favor acquisition within domestic markets.

The institutional environment has been described by three pillars, the first of which is the regulatory, which describes the formal institutions above (Scott, 2014). The other two pillars are formed as informal institutions and described as the normative pillar and the cultural-cognitive pillar. The normative pillar describes things as they have always usually been done—i.e. the "norm", usually formed via historical interactions and (cultural) traditions. With M&A activities the normative pillar suggests that organizations copy other reputable organizations to establish legitimacy.

The cultural-cognitive pillar suggests that it is internalized and taken-for-granted values (with strong cultural influences) that guide alliances and acquisitions. In such cases, understanding and manipulation of the unwritten rules decide the success of alliances and acquisitions.

The resource-based view, as seen in previous chapters, argues that certain firms excel more than others because of the differences in firm-specific capabilities that make alliances and acquisitions work. Firm-specific capabilities can also improve alliance and acquisition performance. Thus, the internal strengths and weaknesses of the organization can strongly determine final decision on whether to borrow or buy and also help with making the decision's implementation successful. Corning, the glass company from upstate New York, is an example of an organization that developed a core competence in managing strategic alliances. It has created many successful joint ventures and alliances, such as Dow Corning. But even that did not help much in its failed venture with Vitro in Mexico, due to conflicts in cultural approaches to the Vitro Corning JV's management.

The VRIO model, introduced earlier as a framework for analyzing the strategic competitive advantages that resources may provide, is also useful to determine the potential of an alliance to create competitive advantage for the organization. First, the advantages of alliances are that they can reduce the risks, costs and uncertainties of a new venture, because you can share these with another organization or entity. They can allow for access to complementary assets and provide learning opportunities that can lead to future growth via the real options path mentioned in Chapter 11. However, a major disadvantage of alliances is that you might choose the wrong partner, due to lack of knowledge in the foreign context. Due to information asymmetry (i.e., the partner knows more than you do about the foreign market and opportunities and threats therein), this may also lead potentially to opportunistic behavior. So, trust becomes important.

Partners can also potentially learn from you, so the flip side of the real options strategy can work in their favor and, ultimately, nurture competition. That is, via a strategic alliance, you may create a future competitor in your original partner! (Note that the propensity towards trusting someone and opportunistic behavior can vary across cultures, so that this issue can be evaluated from the cultural perspective too. Cultures that are more likely to be trusting from the beginning of a new relationship may be more open to alliances but also more vulnerable to opportunistic behavior by partners.)

We can recognize that alliances can be envisioned as a resource or asset of the organization, so the VRIO model might help determine the best option to take. Recall the basic elements of VRIO:

Value: All alliances must create value. To truly derive benefits from alliances, managers need to foster trust with partners yet be on guard against opportunism. To create value via the real option strategy, the investments made in the foreign market must be in real operations, as opposed to just financial capital. Thus, learning—the basis for the real option strategy's success—can take place. Note that nearly 70 percent of acquisitions fail, and in acquisitions the shareholders of target firms are often the benefactors (i.e., the share price of the acquired versus the acquirer usually goes up; acquirer prices often drop!). This suggests that the market often does not see any real value in acquisitions.

Rarity: Relational (or collaborative) capabilities are important to strategic alliance success. This ability to manage inter-firm relationships is often seen as rare. However, acquisitions add value only if the acquired organization possesses rare and unique skills to enhance the overall strategy of the organization, so much will depend on the rarity of these unique skills. Alliances (as general things) are not rare in and of themselves, but the ability to successfully manage them—the true underlying capability or resource—may be rare, and the specific pairing can be considered rare!

Imitability: Alliances make it easier to imitate firm-specific capabilities. Trust and understanding between allies are difficult to imitate. Firms with good post-acquisition integration are difficult to imitate. Again, a specific pairing of compatible partners can be considered non-substitutable.

Organization: Following the previous logic, certain successful alliances are organized in a manner that makes replication difficult. Merged firms must be organized to reap the benefits of the acquisition while minimizing the costs. This requires both strategic and organizational matches or fit. Strategic fit is the effective matching of complementary strategic capabilities. Organizational fit is the similarity in cultures, systems and structures between two or more firms.

On average, the performance of acquiring firms does not improve after acquisition. The only identifiable group of winners in most acquisitions is the shareholders of target firms, who experience, on average, a 25 percent increase in their stock value. This is due to an acquisition premium, which is the difference between the acquisition price and the market value of the target firm.

There are various types of motives for M&A activity that can be explained from either the institutional or resource-based perspectives (Peng, 2016). The first type, synergistic motives, are legitimate strategic reasons for implementing the M&A strategy. Institutionally, they are a response to the institutional structures of the foreign landscape, such as the requirement for FDI activities when entering a foreign market. From a resource-based perspective, an M&A strategy can help to access complementary assets, leverage core competences and build market power for the organization.

The second type, hubristic motives, are based on reasonings that may be untrue, such as having the capability to better manage an acquisition than one's competitors or that M&As are necessary just to keep up with the rest of the industry's behavior. Institutionally, companies follow a herd mentality and may jump on the M&A activity bandwagon. Resource-wise, managers may trick themselves into believing that they have the capabilities to make M&As successful (often this stems from mere overconfidence in their true abilities).

A final type of motivation for M&A activity, managerial motives, is purely based on the benefits that accrue to management. This motivation is potentially insidious, as it is based on the self-interest of top management to grow the organization for the sake of growth alone. This is often due to the fact that larger organizations pay higher salaries and benefits to their top management, and more power in general accumulates to top management as an organization becomes larger. The latter two motives are considered less reasonable and suffer from the principal–agent problem of management—when mismatches occur between the owner's (principal) and manager's (agent) true goals. This may also explain the high rate of M&As, despite their dismal record of failure.

The two final motivations can be found in the research illustrating the problems associated with the failure of acquisitions. These failures can be identified in two phases: Before the M&A strategy is implemented and once the M&A takes place. Pre-acquisition glitches (before the M&A strategy is implemented) often involve overpaying for the target organization. This is due to the information asymmetry issues, in terms of the pricing and true valuation of the target organization. Hubris and managerial motives can lead to overestimations of the value proposition of the M&A as well as poor fit of the target within the existing corporation. Lack of knowledge of the foreign market and institutions and nationalistic political trends can be daunting to overcome.

Post-acquisition issues are most relevant to our discussion in terms of implementing foreign entry strategy, as they involve failure in integrating the organizations. This is often due to misalignments involving both organizational and national culture. The combination of these levels and the number of stakeholders needed to be managed is incredibly complex. Thus, one will want to review the factors explored in earlier chapters on national and organizational cultures when contemplating foreign M&A activity. The models of Hofstede and Trompenaars and the CAGE model may all be relevant to analyzing the potential for success in integrating organizations across national borders. This will depend on both the organization being analyzed and the home and foreign market cultures of the region you are analyzing. Ultimately, the more information and analysis you can generate, the better the probability of both making the right decision about foreign M&A activity and managing such activity after the integration (i.e., after acquisition).

When to Implement a Borrow Strategy when Entering a New Foreign Market

As we have seen, depending upon the situation, using a borrow strategy of working with a partner might be preferable to a buy strategy of acquisition (or greenfield operations). Stephen Tallman and Oded Shenkar (1994) have come up with a simple three-stage managerial decision model of international cooperative venture formation. Figure 12.1 depicts the flow of the model. The first stage is to determine whether your organization's growth can be achieved through market transactions, acquisitions or alliances. The first two can be riddled with complications. For example, the organization has to confront competitive challenges independently and ad hoc to grow via purely market transactions. The disadvantages of acquisitions mentioned earlier may make alliances a better option. In stage two, the organization must

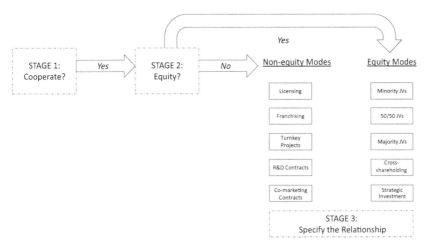

Figure 12.1 Deciding which borrow or buy strategy to utilize

Source: Adapted from Tallman & Shenkar (1994)

decide whether to take a non-equity-based contract approach or an equity-based approach in implementing the strategy. Recall, equity relationships allow organizations to learn tacit capabilities and control certain joint activities but they are also more expensive and riskier. In stage three, the organization specifies a definitive format based on the choices made in stage two.

In implementing the specific market entry format, four factors may influence alliance performance: (1) equity, (2) learning and experience, (3) nationality and (4) relational capabilities. Equity allows for more control and telegraphs that the organization is committed to the strategy. Thus, a greater equity stake can signal commitment and result in greater performance by the alliance. However, the organization also needs to avoid strategic overcommitment or lock-in. The better the learning ability of the organization, the more potential for success, particularly when the goal is to assimilate into the new culture and begin more organic growth for the organization. Nationality, of course, is important, as differences in national cultures and legal institutions ultimately affect the management and potential success of the alliance. Finally, the relational capabilities of the organizations involved can influence the probability of successful alliance performance.

As we saw in Chapter 11, if more control is needed in a strategic alliance situation then acquisitions (or the outright buying of the other organization) might be in order. Colgate's acquisition of Hawley and Hazel in China and its Darlie toothpaste is a case in point. Careful negotiation of managerial rights is needed when partnering within a strategic alliance. Ultimately, experienced lawyers and consultants for the region you are analyzing will need to be consulted to make sure that all legal and political issues are covered.

References

Peng, M. (2016). *GLOBAL3*. New York: Cengage Learning.
Scott, W. R. (2014). *Institutions and organizations: Ideas, interests, and identities*. Thousand Oaks, CA: Sage.
Tallman, S., & Shenkar, O. (1994). A managerial decision model of international cooperative venture formation. *Journal of International Business Studies, 25*(1): 91–113.

Appendix: Suggested Assignments and Project Idea

Semester Project

Global Strategy Team Project

As mentioned in the book's Preface, I use a major term project in my international management course in which students develop a strategic foreign market plan and the implementation protocols for said plan. This primer was a direct result of creating material for such a team effort.

In this Appendix, I provide brief overviews of the assignments that culminate in the master foreign market entry plan and presentation that my students complete utilizing the primer as the conceptual basis for their effort. Although the course assignment is done as a team project, it can be done as a solo project. Thus, any readers keen on using a structured approach can utilize the models and concepts explained in the book to inform their own strategic analysis and create a final report on their own based on these assignments.

The original intent of such a project was for my students to experience the process of developing a global strategic plan for an organization over the semester. During the first week of classes, I usually form students into teams of three to five individuals. The team then chooses an organization that is publicly owned or operated (this is usually because there is ample data publicly available about its operations, but anyone running his or her own private company, with the appropriate information, can undertake the same exercise). Again, to make things feasible with as few headaches as possible,

I suggest to students that the organization should be in a clearly identifiable business or operation (i.e., no holding companies or multi-business corporations). This organization will usually be a publicly listed company but the teams may choose a not-for-profit or private as well (should the team have access to appropriate information for the strategic analysis). The final choice is run by me for final approval and to ensure feasibility. Examples of organizations analyzed include Make-a-Wish, Toyota, Amazon, Ansys and Kellogg, among many others.

Essentially, the teams do a strategic analysis and provide the recommendations for implementing the global expansion of the organization chosen. Work on subsections of the project constitute deliverables for each week of the course. Periodic reporting of the teams' findings to the class are done as the semester progresses.

Deliverables for the project consist of (but are not limited to):

(1) Internal evaluation of the organization
(2) Evaluation and comparisons of potential global expansion (i.e., country comparisons)
(3) Global industry analysis
(4) Stakeholder impact analysis
(5) Mission statement
(6) Country culture report
(7) Entry implementation plans (including org structure, HR and market entry plans)

At the end of the course the teams present the final recommendations on the global strategy of the chosen organization to the class. They also submit a final report with the entire strategic analysis. The 12th assignment is the culmination of the previous 11 and can be found as the last assignment here in this book.

Useful Library and Internet Databases

As I noted in the book's Preface, the book is meant as a guide for further research on specific country and company environment and context. As such, to get the most out of the book requires the readers to do further research for the particular situation they are studying. As such, I list a few databases and internet sites that can be useful to that end. Some are free, others are often offered via an institutional subscription at your university or public library. Of course, practitioners using the book to develop their own strategies can use their internal sources for much data, as well as external sources for environment trends and industry characteristics.

Industry and Company

- IBISWorld—invaluable for industry and sector market information
- Mergent Intellect and/or Mergent Online—for company information

Country Information

- *Political Risk Yearbook*—analysis of the country and its climate for business; includes five-year forecasts under different scenarios
- Export.gov—especially for market intelligence on specific countries

Both Business and Country Data

- ABI/Inform
- Business Source Premier

These are similar databases but cover different sets of articles (with overlap). They include peer-reviewed journals, newspapers, magazines, trade publications, newswires, etc. There is tons of stuff here. Search for an individual company to find current news or do a more complicated search like, "Brazil" AND "Risk Report", in ABI and you'll get Fitch's analysis. You can do that for just about any country. Often more up to date, but not as in depth, as the *Political Risk Yearbook*. But, like any wide-coverage database, you often must be pretty specific in your search, and even then you'll have to sort out some junk.

Country Culture Websites

- www.hofstede-insights.com
- www2.thtconsulting.com
- https://globeproject.com/

Assignment #1

Determine Organization to Study

Objective: Determine via team discussion and internet research which organization the team will study throughout the semester.

Deliverable: Organization's description.

Instructions: With your team, discuss which industry and organization you will study. Using the internet and online library resources such as Compustat, find out information on the organization, such as what business or operations it is in, what countries it currently operates within and what functions are globalized already.

Assignment #2

PESTEL Analyses

Objective: Determine two countries where your chosen organization is not already located and create a PESTEL Analysis of the two countries plus one for the home country. (If your organization is established in most countries, you may choose two that make sense to analyze in a comparison to determine the one that is more worthy of resource deployments.)

Deliverable: PESTEL analyses of the three countries (two countries plus home country).

Instructions: From assignment #1 you have assessed what countries the organization is not currently located or conducting business within. From the list of countries not already located or conducting business within, choose two to study. These may be from two different regions of the world (Algeria versus Belarus) or close regional players (e.g., Poland and the Czech Republic). Using the PESTEL framework from Chapter 2, create a PESTEL analysis of the two countries. Also create a PESTEL model of the home country, by determining the location of the headquarters or country of origin of the chosen organization.

Assignment #3

Global Industry Five Forces Analysis

Objective: Create a five forces analysis of the industry that the organization operates in.

Deliverable: Five forces industry analysis.

Instructions: Determine, and then define by describing the main offerings, what main industry the organization operates in. Using the five forces model described in Chapter 2, create an evaluation of the strength of each of the five forces, plus any complementors for the organization's main industry.

Assignment #4

Internal Factor Evaluation

Objective: Determine the strengths and weaknesses of the organization using the RBV tools described in Chapter 3.

Deliverable: Audit of strengths and weaknesses with internal factor evaluation matrix.

Instructions: With your team, determine the top ten strengths and weaknesses (each) of the organization. Operationalize these as the presence of, and lack thereof, resources or capabilities of the organization. It may be helpful to use the five forces model of assignment #3 to determine what weaknesses might exist given the industry that the organization is in (i.e., the lack of expertise needed for a specific industry, such as brewing in beer).

Assignment #5

Global SSIA and Mission Statement

Objective: Create a strategic stakeholder impact analysis and subsequent stakeholder-focused mission statement.

Deliverable: SSIA table (see Chapter 4 for an example of the elements needed) and stakeholder-focused mission statement.

Instructions: With your team, determine the key internal and external stakeholders for your organization. Be as exhaustive as possible and break down the stakeholder (S/H) group into relevant detailed parts. For example, if your company is an R&D-focused company, you should separate the R&D employees from non-R&D employees. Use Chapter 4 as a basis for the elements in the SSIA table that you generate—i.e., make sure you cover the interests/concerns, claims and strategic challenges of each S/H group.

From the subsequent ranking of the SSIA then create a stakeholder-focused mission statement by focusing on the top S/H groups and incorporating the main strategic thrust of the organization (i.e., what the organization's main goal is and how it will achieve it).

Assignment #6

Global TOWS Analysis

Objective: Create a TOWS matrix using the EFE and IFE matrices developed earlier for the two countries being considered. Choose the most promising mini-strategy/tactic to implement based on the logic of the mission statement developed earlier.

Deliverable: TOWS matrix with at least five mini-strategies/tactics per quadrant. Declaration of the most promising mini-strategy/tactic to implement, along with logic for choice.

Instructions: With your team, you will use the IFE and EFE matrices developed earlier to create five mini-strategies for each TOWS quadrant based on the instructions within Chapter 4. After creating the mini-strategies/tactics per quadrant and listing/charting at least five good ones, your team will argue which one to choose based on how it best links to the mission statement developed earlier. Do this for both countries being considered. Once chosen, the team will craft a rationale for choosing each mini-strategy/tactic.

Assignment #7

CAGE Model Analysis

Objective: Create CAGE models for three countries, including the home base; choose the best option for expansion.

Deliverable: CAGE analysis comparing the three countries. Best option for global expansion.

Instructions: With your team, you will use the CAGE model to compare the two countries chosen to examine, along with the home country of the organization chosen. Write a rationale to explain which country seems to be less "distant" from the home country. After this, compare the chosen TOWS mini-strategies from the last exercise and determine which country and which strategy the team will go forth and implement. This decision will be the basis for the rest of the exercises about implementation issues on which we will work.

Assignment #8

Communication–Culture–Negotiation Profile

Objective: Create communication–culture–negotiation profile.

Deliverable: Communication–culture–negotiation profile for chosen country.

Instructions: For the country chosen from earlier exercises your team will create a profile of the important culture aspects, utilizing the major frameworks from Chapters 6 and 7. Using the cultural data from this analysis, your team can create a recommendation for the negotiation stance and negotiation practices that would be most useful for the cultural background of the chosen country (i.e., given your home country, what important cultural and communication differences will need to be taken into account when negotiating your deal?).

Assignment #9

Organizational Structure Analysis

Objective: Create a potential organizational structure plan for the strategy chosen.

Deliverable: Organizational structure plan for the strategy chosen.

Instructions: Taking into account the communication–culture–negotiation profile from the previous assignment, develop a potential organizational structure plan for the strategy chosen. The team should use information from Chapter 8 to develop the plan. Keep in mind that the plan may change (as they often do) when later decisions about the most appropriate human resources and entry mode / strategies are made.

Assignment #10

International Human Resource Management Analysis

Objective: Create an IHRM plan for the country you plan to enter.

Deliverable: A plan for staffing your foreign subsidiary based on the culture of the country chosen as well as the most appropriate global strategic orientation.

Instructions: Using the concepts from Chapter 9 and Chapter 10, and, specifically, the IHRM model of practices shown in Figure 10.1, your team will create an IHRM plan that would suit the culture and recommended global strategic orientation of your organization. In your plan, you should discuss the leadership characteristics that would be most impactful for the culture of the country chosen. The plan will also cover recommendations of the five practices of the HR process: (1) recruitment and selection; (2) training and development; (3) performance appraisal; (4) compensation; and (5) labor relations.

Assignment #11

Vehicles for Market Entry Analysis

Objective: Create an entry mode plan for the country you plan to enter.

Deliverable: An entry mode plan for entering the chosen foreign market based on the cultural and legal aspects of the country chosen, as well as the most appropriate global strategic orientation and managerial issues specific to your organization.

Instructions: Using the concepts from Chapters 11 and 12, create a plan for entering the chosen foreign market that would suit the business environment of that market and managerial issues associated with the build, borrow or buy model. Note that this will depend on the legal/administrative aspects of the country as well as the cultural. In addition, issues of managerial control and costs as well as the internal strengths of your organization will need to be applied.

Assignment #12

Full Market Entry Report

Here is an example of the final report and presentation I have my students complete in the course on international strategy and management that I teach at Penn State. One can imagine utilizing the same outline to present a report to the board of directors or senior management at the organization when discussing possible foreign opportunities. As such, with tweaking, it can be used in a multitude of settings depending on the reader's needs.

Objective: Create a full report on the global market entry strategy developed over the semester.

Deliverable: Fully re-analyzed report of assignments #1 through #11 based on the updates and changes made over the course of the semester. Presentation of said report and a professional-level document of the report (to be submitted for grading).

Instructions: Your team will create a report of the entire work done this semester—written in a concise and focused document (10–20 single-spaced and 12-pt font pages). You will also present the final report to class.

Note that previous sections of your report will have changed based on the feedback during the semester and changes that may have to accompany the final strategy chosen. The report will have the following sections:

(1) Executive summary
(2) Strategic need for globalization (Chapter 1)
   (a) Give the rationale behind the reasons for your organization to globalize
(3) Internal analysis of organization (Chapter 3)
   (a) List ten main strengths and weaknesses conceptualized as important resources or capabilities for your organization—either present (i.e., strengths) or absent (i.e., weaknesses)
   (b) Illustrate your strategic stakeholder impact analysis with focus on the major stakeholders
(4) External analysis of target country (Chapter 2; Chapter 6; Chapter 7)
   (a) Give a PESTEL analysis of environmental trends within the home and target countries
   (b) Discuss briefly the major cultural aspects of the target country (focus particularly on those aspects that might pose issues due to home-country conflicts …)
   (c) CAGE model comparison of home versus target country (cover differences and similarities of countries and potential problematic issues there arising …)
   (d) Generate ten major positive and negative trends in the country (i.e., threats (negative trends, like worsening economy) and opportunities (positive trends, like increasing wages) and remember to express these as trends! These will come from the PESTEL and CAGE analyses above.
(5) TOWS matrix (Chapter 4)
   (a) Give the major TOWS strategy/tactic (developed based on sections 3 and 4 above) chosen to focus on for the foreign market entry
(6) Global strategic orientation (Chapter 5)
   (a) Tabulate the suggested global strategic orientation for your organization based on the major offering for the organization
(7) Entry mode (Chapter 11)
   (a) Remember to describe the rationale for the chosen entry mode by using data from your analyses above to back the decision up (e.g., are

there laws and regulations deterring a specific mode? Does it suit the home organizational culture and business acumen? Etc.)

(8) Organizational structure plan (Chapter 8)

    (a) Again, back the decision up with facts like strategic and cultural fit, etc.

(9) Negotiation plan (Chapter 9)

    (a) Ditto as per section 8.

(10) IHRM Plan (Chapter 9; Chapter 10)

    (a) Ditto as per section 8. Remember that there is no right or wrong decision; only better and worse; based on the rationale used. In practice, your decision will need to stand the test of the marketplace, and the better planned out it is, the more probable the success. As such, the quality of the analysis and the "reasonable-ness" (i.e., logic) of the fit with your final decision are important factors.

Index

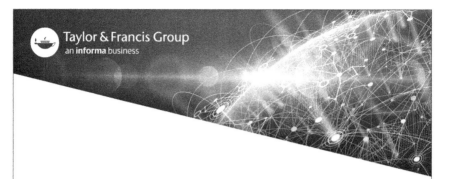